P9-EMB-834

# Promoting
# Reflective Thinking
# in Teachers

# Promoting Reflective Thinking in Teachers

## in Teachers

*50* Action Strategies

Germaine L. Taggart | Alfred P. Wilson

**CORWIN PRESS**
A SAGE Publications Company
Thousand Oaks, California

Copyright © 2005 by Corwin Press

All rights reserved. When forms and sample documents are included, their use is authorized only by educators, local school sites, and/or noncommercial or nonprofit entities who have purchased the book. Except for that usage, no part of this book may be reproduced or utilized in any form or by any means, electronic or mechanical, including photocopying, recording, or by any information storage and retrieval system, without permission in writing from the publisher.

*For information:*

Corwin Press
A Sage Publications Company
2455 Teller Road
Thousand Oaks, California 91320
www.corwinpress.com

Sage Publications Ltd.
1 Oliver's Yard
55 City Road
London EC1Y 1SP
United Kingdom

Sage Publications India Pvt. Ltd.
B-42, Panchsheel Enclave
Post Box 4109
New Delhi 110 017 India

Printed in the United States of America

*Library of Congress Cataloging-in-Publication Data*

Taggart, Germaine L.
Promoting reflective thinking in teachers: 50 action strategies/by Germaine L. Taggart, Alfred P. Wilson.— 2nd ed.
    p. cm.
Includes bibliographical references and index.
ISBN 1-4129-0963-5 (cloth) — ISBN 1-4129-0964-3 (pbk.)
   1. Teachers—Training of. 2. Teachers—In-service training.
3. Thought and thinking. 4. Reflective teaching. I. Wilson, Alfred P. II. Title.
LB1707.T24 2005
370'.71'1—dc22                                    2004027697

This book is printed on acid-free paper.

05   06   07   08   09   10   9   8   7   6   5   4   3   2   1

| | |
|---|---|
| *Acquisitions Editor:* | Faye Zucker |
| *Editorial Assistant:* | Gem Rabanera |
| *Production Editor:* | Beth Bernstein |
| *Copy Editor:* | Teresa Herlinger |
| *Typesetter:* | C&M Digitals (P) Ltd. |
| *Proofreader:* | Richard Moore |
| *Indexer:* | Molly Hall |
| *Cover Designer:* | Rose Storey |
| *Graphic Designer:* | Lisa Miller |

# Contents

# Preface

*If change is to occur, reflective thinking must become a taken-for-granted lens through which preservice teachers conceptualize their practice.*
—Ross and Hannay (1986)

**P**romoting *Reflective Thinking in Teachers: 50 Action Strategies* provides teacher educators and staff developers, hereafter referred to as facilitators, with strategies to enhance the reflective thinking abilities of preservice and inservice educators. *Reflective thinking* refers to the process of making informed and logical decisions, then assessing the consequences of those decisions. The guide was developed on the premise that reflective thinking is required for effective teaching. Strategies for reflective thinking are approached at three levels: technical, contextual, and dialectical. Within each level, strategies have been field-tested with populations of preservice and inservice teachers. The guide has been reviewed by teacher educators across the nation to verify and validate its usefulness.

Three major goals supported the construction of this document. One was to develop a practical guide to be used by facilitators to augment the reflective thinking of practitioners.

The second was to design a document that is nonlinear in nature. Information gleaned from teacher educators in a nationwide telephone survey indicated the need for a guide with strategies that could be incorporated into existing course work as well as provide a general guideline for staff development in a seminar or workshop format. The successful use of this guide is not dependent on use in a lockstep, sequential fashion. Rather, the user is encouraged to select desired strategies that are pertinent to the needs of particular practitioners.

A third goal was to provide several assessment strategies that would facilitate determination of a practitioner's reflective thinking level so that a benchmark could be established and growth in reflective thinking determined.

Each chapter focuses on a major component of enhancing reflective thinking of practitioners.

# ORGANIZATION OF THE GUIDE

Chapters are arranged with a logical progression in mind. Chapter 1 provides a basis for introducing reflective thinking to practitioners. A reflective thinking model is presented to show the cyclical nature of reflective thinking and to discern the steps of reflection. The process is graphically displayed as well as explained in writing. Three levels of reflective thinking—technical, contextual, and dialectical—are presented along with characteristics of practitioners who are functioning reflectively at each level. The chapter is intended to provide facilitators with background information regarding reflective thinking. Strategies and support materials found in this chapter may be used to provide background knowledge to practitioners on both the process of reflection and reflective levels.

A final section of Chapter 1 deals with preparing a plan of action for continued growth in reflective thinking. Joyce and Showers (1995) stress that learning activities should be extended over a period of time, with feedback and sessions spaced at intervals throughout the development process. A strategic plan of action will allow practitioners to use what has been learned about reflection to create a long-range plan that incorporates existing and newly acquired schemata and continual feedback. Through such a plan, the natural tendency of adults to problem solve and to resolve discrepancies between what is and what should be addressed can be enhanced.

The authors assume that when facilitating reflection, certain materials will be in place. An overhead projector should be in the session location as well as materials such as Vis-á-Vis® pens, note cards, chart paper, newsprint, and masking tape. Many activities require clear transparencies to be used, as teams report information produced from their discussions. Other required materials have been kept to a minimum to enhance portability of the tasks. Facilitators may also choose to adapt guide materials to emerging technologies, such as the use of computers and projection panels or personal data assistants (PDAs). Locations for sessions should support teaming activities. It is suggested that tables and chairs be used to provide a less formal structure than the traditional lecturer-audience room format.

Chapter 2 focuses on assessment of reflective thinking. Consideration of a practitioner's current reflective level is paramount for providing individuals with benchmarks for determining reflective growth. An attribute profile is provided to be used in conjunction with other reflective thinking assessments to assist the facilitator and practitioners in determining levels of reflection. The use of the attribute profile will be one of the first activities used in course work or seminars. Practitioners should be assured that the profile is one component of many for obtaining baseline levels of reflection. There is no risk to taking the assessment. There are no correct or incorrect answers.

Strategies used to promote reflective thinking are the focus of Chapters 3 through 9. Strategies include observational learning; reflective journals; practicum activities, such as reflective teaching and microteaching; mental-model strategies, such as metaphors and repertory grids; narrative strategies, such as story, autobiographical sketches, and case study; establishing technology-enhanced learning communities; and action research. For each strategy presented, an explanation is given along with reflective activities and questions. Action assignments, suggestions for success, journaling for reflective growth, and extended readings are provided to assist the facilitator in guiding practitioners through higher levels of reflective thinking. Strategies are intended to be selected based on general reflective levels, interest levels, and the facilitator's knowledge of the skill levels of the practitioners. Not all of the strategies within each category are intended to be used during any one session. Strategies generally require little direct instruction by the facilitator. Teaming of practitioners to obtain a product for discussion, application of the product created, and promotion of discussion by the facilitator are essential.

Objectives are provided for the facilitator to help focus the preparations toward presenting reflective thinking models, assessments, and strategies. Handouts and transparencies for each task are provided in each chapter.

## USES FOR THE GUIDE

The intention of creating the reflective thinking guide was that it be used by staff developers as a resource from which to draw activities for seminars on reflective thinking strategies. It may also be used by teacher educators in university-based course work as a main or supplementary text to enhance reflection in preservice teachers.

The reflective thinking guide can be used by teacher educators in several ways. First, the guide may serve as the primary material for use in seminars or workshops to enhance the reflective thinking of practitioners. As a staff development guide, activities from the text may be selected to create a cohesive program that is 10 to 15 hours in length. As was stated earlier, to provide the practitioner with the most practice, reflection time, and meaningful feedback, it is recommended by the authors that the time frame be spread out over a 4- to 6-week period, perhaps using five 3-hour sessions or four 4-hour sessions.

Second, the guide is designed for courses that correlate to participation of preservice teachers in field settings. When used in this context, activities found within the guide may be selected to support a particular activity or objective for each field experience. The activities may be incorporated into lessons focusing on such topics as classroom management or inclusion, leading the practitioners through a sequential process toward becoming more reflective in their observations and practice.

Journaling is an important component of the reflective thinking process and should be encouraged by the facilitator. A variety of assessment techniques are also provided to assist in determining baseline reflective thinking levels and subsequent growth in reflective thinking.

Third, course work designed to prepare preservice teachers for imminent field experiences may constitute a setting for use of the reflective thinking guide. Activities found in Chapter 1 may be used to introduce practitioners to the reflective thinking model and process. Also, activities such as "Observing

Effective Questioning" and "Formatting a Journal Entry" from Chapters 3 and 4, respectively, may be used to prepare practitioners for observational learning or journaling.

It is the sincere desire of the authors that this reflective thinking guide provide facilitators of preservice and inservice practitioners with an easy reference to strategies that fit the needs of both facilitators and practitioners. Attention is focused on adaptability in terms of time constraints and materials, value of strategies to promote increased reflection, and ease in selection of components to support existing course work and provide tasks for seminars to enhance reflective thinking.

# About the Authors

**Germaine L. Taggart** is Associate Professor in the College of Education at Fort Hays State University, Hays, Kansas. She has taught students from kindergarten through Grade 12 in public schools in Kansas. She received her BS and MS degrees in Elementary Education from Pittsburg State University, her EdS in Educational Administration from Fort Hays State University, and her EdD in Educational Administration from Kansas State University.

She teaches mathematics and science methods courses, has helped develop and continues to work with TEAM: Links for Learning (a field-based preservice program), and provides staff development on a consultant basis for school districts in western Kansas.

Dr. Taggart is married to R. Bruce Taggart. They have two children, Travis and Kelsey, and one granddaughter, MacKenzie, and they reside in Hays, Kansas.

**Alfred P. Wilson** is Professor Emeritus of Educational Administration at Kansas State University. He has served as a public school teacher and administrator and as a university faculty member and administrator in the states of Nevada, Utah, Montana, New Mexico, Idaho, and Kansas. He received his doctorate from Utah State University in 1969.

He is the author or coauthor of more than 25 books and monographs and 100 articles and research papers. He has been consultant to more than 200 school districts in 42 states, 20 state departments and regional service centers for education, 15 community colleges and universities, and a broad variety of organizations.

Dr. Wilson has been an active member and leader in many organizations, including the American Research Association, Phi Delta Kappa, the American Association of School Administrators, and the American Management Association.

# Becoming a Reflective Teacher

*An empowered teacher is a reflective decision maker who finds joy in learning and in investigating the teaching/learning process—one who views learning as construction and teaching as a facilitating process to enhance and enrich development.*

—Fosnot (1989, p. xi)

---

### *Chapter Objectives*

**The facilitator will**

- Differentiate among the technical, contextual, and dialectical modes of reflective thinking
- Recognize and be able to describe the cyclical process of reflective thinking
- Be provided with tasks to help practitioners use the reflective thinking process
- Be provided with tasks assisting in the recognition of characteristics of practitioners functioning in each of the three reflective thinking modes
- Support preparation of a plan for continued growth in reflective thinking

---

Reflective thinking is the process of making informed and logical decisions on educational matters, then assessing the consequences of those decisions. Campbell-Jones and Campbell-Jones (2002) describe reflection as an "inner dialogue with oneself whereby a person calls forth experiences, beliefs, and perceptions" (p. 134). Risko, Roskos, and Vukelich (2002) continue the process explanation by adding that the dialogue should both inform and transform knowledge and action. Scholars of reflective thinking have categorized it according to the mode of thinking or the process an individual progresses through to reach a level of reflection that complements both the context of the situation and the background the individual brings to the episode. This chapter will assist the facilitator with background knowledge for discussing both the modes and process of reflective thinking, tasks to use with practitioners desiring to enhance reflective thinking ability, and a format to aid practitioners in preparation of a plan for continued growth in reflective thinking.

## MODES OF REFLECTIVE THINKING

One way of manifesting the characteristics of reflective thinking is through modes of delivery. Scholars differ on the hierarchical nature of reflective thinking but generally agree on three modes or levels: technical, contextual, and dialectical. The Reflective Thinking Pyramid (see Figure 1.1) provides an example of the three levels.

### Technical

Van Manen (1977) refers to the initial level of reflective thinking as *technical rationality*. Van Manen serves as a model for Lasley (1992) and Grimmett, MacKinnon, Erickson, and Riecken (1990) in that the first level of reflection deals with methodological problems and theory development to achieve objectives. Valli (1990, 1997) also refers to the first level as technical rationality but differs by positing that technical rationality is a nonreflective level. Valli's second level, practical decision making, adds reflection to the technical aspects of teaching. Collier (1999) simply categorizes technical reflection as reaction.

Practitioners reflecting at the technical level function with minimal schemata from which to draw when dealing with problems. Getting through lessons and using instructional management approaches are short-term measures that may be reflected on in terms of meeting outcomes. The individual, often isolated, episodes are building blocks for developing the professional repertoire needed to reflectively handle nonroutine problems. Many novice teachers are thought to function at a technical level based on a lack of schemata in dealing with educative problems.

Outcomes for practitioners reflecting at a technical level may involve appropriate selection and implementation of lessons to achieve objectives. The objectives are not problematic nor does the practitioner deliberate on the context of the situation. Acquisition of skills and technical knowledge is important, as are methodological awareness and ability to implement a preset lesson. Technical practitioners may be transitioning into linking theory development to practice and identification of the relevancy of activities and objectives. Practitioners need to be making observations and processing information to move toward solving problems and testing possible solutions for decision validity.

**Figure 1.1** Reflective Thinking Pyramid

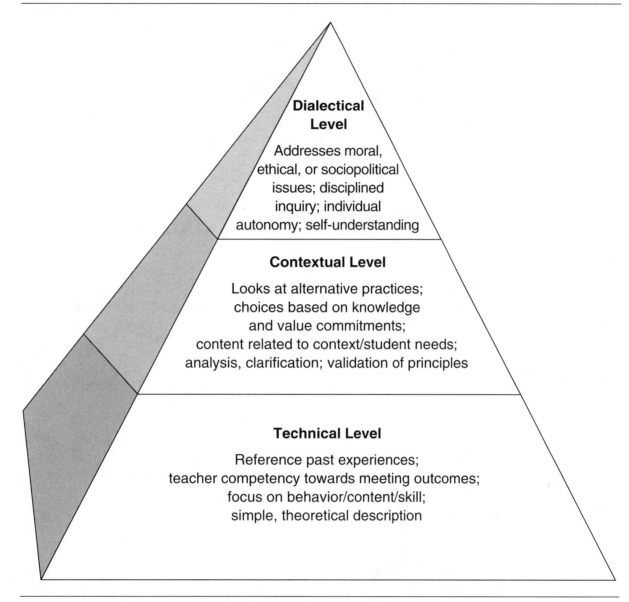

**Dialectical Level**

Addresses moral, ethical, or sociopolitical issues; disciplined inquiry; individual autonomy; self-understanding

**Contextual Level**

Looks at alternative practices; choices based on knowledge and value commitments; content related to context/student needs; analysis, clarification; validation of principles

**Technical Level**

Reference past experiences; teacher competency towards meeting outcomes; focus on behavior/content/skill; simple, theoretical description

Copyright © 2005 by Corwin Press. All rights reserved. Reprinted from *Promoting Reflective Thinking in Teachers: 50 Action Strategies*, by Germaine Taggart. Thousand Oaks, CA: Corwin Press, www.corwinpress.com. Reproduction authorized only for the local school site or nonprofit organization that has purchased this book.

Facilitators working with practitioners functioning at a technical level should provide genuine, continuous experiences; observational learning instruction; and thoughtful discussion of problems and possible solutions. Experimentation and application of solutions with clear explanations and meaningful activities are also important. Sessions should provide necessary pedagogy, content, and theory, and then foster use, examination, and analysis of instructional and management approaches. Knowledge of student characteristics will also be helpful to the technical practitioner in being able to reflect on problems faced in a field placement.

## Contextual

A second level of reflection (Collier, 1999; Grimmett et al., 1990; Lasley, 1992; Van Manen, 1977) involves reflections regarding clarification of and elaboration on underlying assumptions and predispositions of classroom practice as well as consequences of strategies used. The contextual mode deals with pedagogical matters as examined relative to a relationship between theory and practice. The nonproblematic nature of the technical level gives way to problems at the contextual level. Problems stem from personal biases resulting from a practitioner's belief system, looking at situations in context, and questioning of practices based on increased pedagogical knowledge and skills. Problems at the contextual level cause practitioners to reflect on the contextual situation, which often leads to better teaching.

An outcome for practitioners reflecting at this level may be understanding concepts, contexts, and theoretical bases for classroom practices, then defending those practices and articulating their relevance to student growth. Self-reflection to interpret and inform practice and establish congruency between theory and practice would be indicative of functioning at a contextual level. Clarification of assumptions and predispositions of practice and consequences helps contextual practitioners assess implications and consequences of actions and beliefs. Through increased practice and theoretical knowledge, practitioners examine competing views relative to consequences and actions, and then begin to develop routines and "rules of thumb." Understanding personal and environmental interactions is also a desired outcome for practitioners functioning at a contextual level.

Facilitators working with practitioners functioning at a contextual level should provide knowledge of situational constraints and external agents that may affect effective teaching. Time for collegial support, input, and discussion should be incorporated into sessions to provide bridges between and among concepts, theories, and practices. Questioning should be used to foster reflection with positive and timely feedback being provided.

## Dialectical

Van Manen's (1977) third and highest level of reflectivity, *critical reflectivity,* deals with the questioning of moral and ethical issues related directly and indirectly to teaching practices. Critical reflectivity is comparable to the dialectical level of Grimmett et al. (1990) and Lasley (1992). At this level, practitioners contemplate ethical and political concerns relative to instructional planning and implementation. Equality, emancipation, caring, and justice are assessed in regard to curriculum planning. Practitioners are concerned with worth of knowledge and social circumstances useful to students without personal bias. The ability to make defensible choices and view an event with open-mindedness is also indicative of reflecting at a dialectical level. Collier (1999) viewed this highest level of reflection as contemplative.

Outcomes for practitioners functioning at the dialectical level relate to looking for and analyzing knowledge systems and theories in context and in relation to one another. Outcomes dealing with critical examination of underlying assumptions, norms, and rules; practicing introspection, open-mindedness, and intellectual responsibility (Dewey, 1933); and questioning moral and ethical issues of teaching, instructional planning, and implementation are all a part of higher aspects of reflection found at the dialectical level.

Concern with worth of knowledge and social consequence should be explored as well as defense of choices using external and internal dialogue. Classroom implications should be extended to society while reflecting on opposing viewpoints and cross-examining issues and practices. Risk taking on the part of the dialectical practitioner in the form of peer review and self-assessment independent of external standards or conditions will help the practitioner at this level achieve self-efficacy and self-actualization. Practitioners are developing expert knowledge and the ability to reconstruct action situations as a means for reviewing the self as teacher, and questioning assumptions previously taken for granted. Examination of contradictions and systematic attempts to resolve issues are probable outcomes.

Facilitators working with practitioners functioning at a dialectical level should provide a forum to assist them in deciding worthiness of actions and analyzing curriculum approaches, case studies, conventional wisdom, and technocratic approaches. Sessions should enable practitioners to look at issues in terms of optimum benefit for students and teacher empowerment. Action research should also be an outcome of reflective thinking at the dialectical level. Other activities may be analyzing stereotypes and biases through narratives and storytelling, practicing affective elements of caring and concern, and reflecting on the role of school climate and on society's role in education.

## THE PROCESS APPROACH

Dewey (1933), Eby and Kujawa (1994), Pugach and Johnson (1990), and Schön (1983) delineate a cyclical process approach to reflective thinking. Figure 1.2 illustrates the reflective thinking process. In each instance, the first step to reflective thinking involves a problem. Dewey refers to such a problem as a *felt difficulty*. Schön uses the term *problematic situation* to identify the initial step of reflection in action.

A second step in the process is to step back from the problem to look at the situation from a third-person perspective so that the problem may be framed or reframed (Clarke, 1995; Pugach & Johnson, 1990; Schön, 1987). Dewey (1933) refers to the stage in which the problem is understood as one of providing location and definition. Eby and Kujawa (1994) dissect the process using components of observation, reflection, data gathering, and consideration of moral principles. These features provide the mental picture of the thought processes entertained by the reflective practitioner in an attempt to define a problem. Also represented at the definition stage are the parallel features of context and schema. The episode is likened to past events in an attempt to make sense of the problem and to search for possible solutions in the reflective thinker's repertoire. Once the reflective practitioner has searched for routine solutions to a possibly nonroutine situation or has devised possible solutions based on reasoning through similar past experiences, predictions are made and possible solutions generated. The solutions are systematically tested with subsequent observation and further experimentation, if needed, and judgments are made relative to the level of success of the intervention. Dewey likened the process to the scientific method.

Evaluation, the next stage in the process, consists of a review of the implementation process and the consequences of the solution. Acceptance or rejection of the solution takes place. If the solution proves successful, the instance may be stored for subsequent retrieval in similar situations or may become routine (Dewey, 1933). If the solution is not successful, the problem may be reframed and the process repeated.

## TECHNIQUES FOR FACILITATING REFLECTIVE ACTIVITIES

A constructivist approach is used in this guide. Piaget (1975) was a proponent of the constructivist view of learning, which advocates learning as a process of change. Through simultaneous processes of assimilation and accommodation, new information is added to an existing repertoire of knowledge. Assimilation is a process by which knowledge is restructured so it can be integrated into an existing schema. Accommodation is the process that allows practitioners to restructure knowledge by making modifications to existing schemata. When knowledge is constructed that correlates to an existing schema, balance or equilibrium occurs.

Two basic principles of constructivism are (a) what a person knows is actively assembled by the learner (Brooks & Brooks, 1993) and (b) learning serves an adaptive function of storage of useful information. The following learning experiences are appropriate for a constructivist program:

- Emphasis on learning as reflective thinking and productivity: A fundamental goal should be the ability to perform relevant tasks in a variety of effective ways
- Context-rich learning: Learning should focus on authentic activities, allow for student collaboration in exploring and evaluating ideas, and provide learning experiences that foster communication and access to real-world examples
- Access to models of the skills appropriate to the learning situation, ideally in an apprenticeship relationship

**Figure 1.2** Reflective Thinking Model

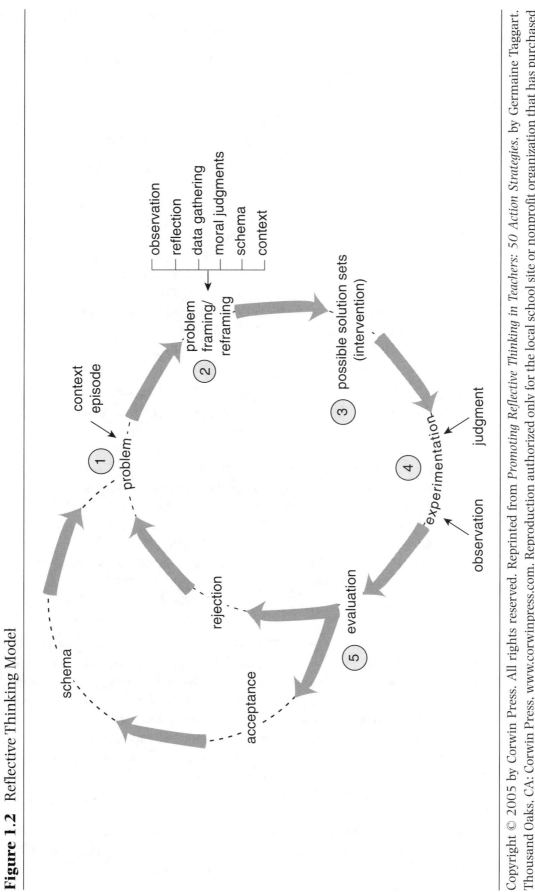

Copyright © 2005 by Corwin Press. All rights reserved. Reprinted from *Promoting Reflective Thinking in Teachers: 50 Action Strategies*, by Germaine Taggart. Thousand Oaks, CA: Corwin Press. www.corwinpress.com. Reproduction authorized only for the local school site or nonprofit organization that has purchased this book.

A constructivist (see Table 1.1), then, is a practitioner who

- Believes all knowledge is constructed or invented by the learner
- Involves learners in active manipulations of meanings, numbers, and patterns
- Believes learning is nonlinear
- Provides students with the tools of empowerment: concepts, heuristic procedures, self-motivation, and reflection
- Believes learning occurs most effectively through guided discovery, meaningful application, and problem solving

By adhering to such an ideal, the facilitator subscribes to the purpose of this guide, a purpose that fosters change; allows learners to progress at a pace indicative of experience, knowledge, and interest; and supports growth in reflective thinking.

The purpose of the book is also supported by existing andragogical knowledge. *Andragogy,* the teaching of adults, is based on several assumptions about adult learners (Knowles, 1990):

- The need to know is strong in adult learners. Benefits, consequences, and risks must be ascertained prior to involvement in the learning situation.
- Self-concept and intellectual responsibility of adult learners lend credence to self-directed learning situations.
- Experiential learning built on the adult learner's past experiences is essential. Group discussion, simulations, and problem-solving activities emphasizing peer collaboration have proven effective with adult learners.
- Readiness to learn is inherent in adult learners.
- Connections to real-life situations and examination of relevancy issues motivate adult learners.
- Adult learners are often intrinsically motivated.

Responsibilities within the facilitative role of the staff developer or teacher educator that augment the andragogical model involve such tasks as presenting the relevance of ideas and concepts, allowing self-directed peer activities and the facilitation of discussion regarding those activities, and using knowledge of previous experiences or examination of an existing schema on which to build current experiences. For these reasons, this guide has been constructed in a nonlinear fashion. A variety of activities for each topic and at each reflective thinking level has been created. Activities are often self-directed peer activities that allow the practitioners to construct their own knowledge, thus supporting intrinsic motivation and relevancy.

Certain techniques for facilitating learning have been supported by research and are used throughout the guide. What follows is a brief description of each technique to aid facilitators in role clarification.

**Table 1.1**    Defining a Constructivist

*A Constructivist . . .*

- Believes all knowledge is constructed or invented by the learner

- Involves learners in active manipulations of meanings, numbers, and patterns

- Believes learning is nonlinear

- Provides students with tools of empowerment: concepts, heuristic procedures, self-motivation, and reflection

- Believes learning occurs most effectively through guided discovery, meaningful application, and problem solving

Reprinted by permission. Adapted from Brooks, I.G. et al. (1993), *In Search of Understanding: The Case for the Constructivist Classroom.* The Association for Supervision and Curriculum Development is a worldwide community of educators advocating sound policies and sharing best practices to achieve the sucess of each learner. To learn more, visit ASCD at www.ascd.org.

## Thinking Aloud

Practitioners learn reflection through the modeling of their mentors. Deliberate and systematic reflection that is visible or audible to practitioners promotes teaching by the very example it sets. Practitioners see reflection when there is a pause in teaching to consider a remark or through the care and effort of a mentor to put observations into verbal thought.

## Discussions

Classroom discussion is a basic teaching tool. *Classroom discussion* is defined in this guide as practitioners creating understanding by exchanging information, opinions, or experiences while working toward a common goal. The facilitator observes and encourages the group's efforts without becoming directly involved. Discussions may take place face-to-face or through technological formats in a synchronous or asynchronous mode.

## Grouping Practices

Grouping of practitioners will vary within the context of the activity objective. Whole-group discussion may be held as well as small-team activities. Individuals will at times prepare a preliminary list of ideas for later discussion within a small team or whole group. Small–team numbers will vary depending on the activity and are generally stated under the procedure section of the activity. Also found in this section are designated ways of sectioning teams and possible ways of determining team roles. Means for determining teams and roles should be considered as suggestions, because factors, such as group numbers and room logistics will affect partitioning of groups by the facilitator.

The facilitator's role within the group is to provide necessary background and directions, establish ground rules, present the assignment, and facilitate the work of the group in meeting the activity objective. Facilitation of an activity involves allowing practitioners to assume responsibility for the group's success. Facilitators should not interject their own ideas, opinions, or information. While practitioners are working in groups, facilitators should move quietly about the room, monitoring but not interrupting. Show by your presence that you are supportive, attentive, and available. Encourage groups having difficulty by suggesting ways of problem solving rather than suggesting solutions.

## Cooperative Learning

Cooperative learning is used widely today at all levels of education (Aronson, Blaney, Stephan, Sikes, & Snapp, 1978; Johnson, Johnson, & Holubec, 1991; Slavin, 1983). It is particularly effective for adult learners. Cooperative learning benefits learners by

- Increasing achievement through collaboration
- Improving relations among diverse learners (gender, age, culture, ethnicity)
- Developing problem-solving skills
- Fostering democratic processes in learning

Practitioners cooperate to complete the learning task. Cooperative learning tasks are set up in a manner where each participant has a role that must be adhered to if the task is to be completed. One example of cooperative learning tasks used in this guide is Task 12 (see Chapter 3), which uses the *jigsaw* technique (Aronson et al., 1978).

As the facilitator, your position is to promote group learning. The facilitator establishes purpose and rules, provides interesting and meaningful tasks, provides direction, and monitors group interaction. Assessment of task completion is necessary both from an academic standpoint and from a social standpoint. Not only must the task be completed well, but all members of the group must cooperate in its completion. Facilitators relate the value of working cooperatively to the practitioners.

Practitioners are expected to be self-directed and apply leadership techniques with the purpose of completing a task in a collaborative setting. They are responsible for the success of the team. Practitioners should be active, accountable, cooperative, and caring. Peer feedback and self-evaluation are important aspects of cooperative learning.

While monitoring cooperative groups, a facilitator needs to be mobile and observant. Groups are monitored for both academic and social success. If intervention is needed within a team, enter the team at eye level, which promotes a sense of equality rather than superiority on the facilitator's part. Provide questioning that prompts the group to return to the task with the least amount of interference.

## Brainstorming

Brainstorming will often be used during task discussions in this guide. A set time limit will be used, with practitioners expressing all the ideas on a given topic within time constraints. All answers are acceptable, the goal being quantity of ideas, uninhibited participation, and uncritical acceptance by team members. A recorder should be chosen prior to the brainstorming activity to write down the ideas of all other members. Questions used in brainstorming are generally literal and open-ended. Guidelines for brainstorming (see Table 1.2) are

- Preset time constraints
- Equality and democracy
- All ideas acceptable; be creative
- Volume of ideas important
- No discussion of ideas
- Risk-free environment
- Designated recorder

## Consensus Building

Consensus building is a logical follow-up activity to brainstorming. After ideas have been generated, discussion is often necessary to decide what ideas best fit the current situation or question. The cardinal rule is that the solution must be acceptable to all team members. The following are consensus guidelines (Harrington-Macklin, 1994; see Table 1.3):

- Topic or idea is placed before the team for discussion.
- Topic is discussed, questions and concerns are raised, data and solution options are presented.
- Team decides whether to try to achieve consensus, how long it will spend, and what it will do if consensus cannot be reached.
- Differences and disagreements, as well as similarities, are explored and encouraged.
- Suggestions and modifications to the original topic are made.
- A new idea is created by the team on the basis of discussion.
- Facilitator checks for consensus.
- If no consensus, facilitator asks for a variation of the idea and tests for consensus again.
- If no consensus can be reached, facilitator suggests stand-aside proposals (trial time period, modified plan).
- Facilitator tests for consensus for stand-aside proposal.

## Buzz Groups

Buzz groups are informal, loosely structured, and small. They are used to break down larger groups into smaller teams, which makes interaction of members less cumbersome. Buzz groups are generally practitioner run. Each team briefly addresses the problem at hand, records ideas, selects a designated reporter, then brings the team's ideas back to the whole group for presentation.

## Role-Playing

Role-playing activities can help to improve understanding by allowing practitioners to think about and discuss the role of the speaker or writer, audience, or subject matter within a problem. The technique helps the facilitator gain insight into the feelings of the practitioners and helps discover what is important to them. Practitioners may be chosen or elect to participate in a particular role. The scenario is set by the facilitator, but the dialogue should be developed spontaneously. Discretion must be used to avoid embarrassment and discomfort.

## Questioning

Effective questioning serves to meet several goals (Heathcote, 1980). Through effective questioning, the facilitator may

- Bring focus to an activity
- Cause group members to reflect on alternatives not otherwise discussed
- Promote identification of issues in more depth
- Control the direction or mood of the practitioners
- Promote beliefs and values clarification
- Deepen insight of practitioners

**Table 1.2**     Guidelines for Brainstorming

- Preset time constraints

- Equality and democracy

- All ideas acceptable; be creative

- Volume of ideas important

- No discussion of ideas

- Risk-free environment

- Designated recorder

Copyright © 2005 by Corwin Press. All rights reserved. Reprinted from *Promoting Reflective Thinking in Teachers: 50 Action Strategies*, by Germaine Taggart. Thousand Oaks, CA: Corwin Press, www.corwinpress.com. Reproduction authorized only for the local school site or nonprofit organization that has purchased this book.

**Table 1.3**     Consensus Guidelines

- Topic or idea is placed before the team for discussion.

- Topic is discussed, questions and concerns raised, and data and solution options presented.

- Team decides whether to achieve consensus, the length of time to spend, and what to do if consensus cannot be reached.

- Differences and disagreements, as well as similarities, are explored and encouraged.

- Suggestions and modifications are made to original topic.

- Discussion by the team follows to create a new idea.

- Facilitator checks for consensus.

- If no consensus, facilitator asks for a variation of the idea and tests for consensus again.

- If no consensus, facilitator suggests stand–aside proposals.

- Facilitator tests for consensus for stand-aside proposal.

Excerpted with permission of the publisher, from *The Team Building Tool Kit*, by Deborah Harrington-Macklin. © 1994 New Directions Management Services, Inc. Published by AMACOM, a division of American Management Association.

Heathcote (1980) also suggests several guidelines for questioning: Effective questions asked by practitioners must be real; help practitioners focus on where they are, what they are doing, and why they are doing it; lead practitioners to wonder about and seek out new information; and move practitioners to reflect on the significance of actions.

There are many kinds of effective questions. Among them are

- Information-seeking questions
- Questions that encourage research
- Questions that supply information
- Questions that require group decision making
- Class-controlling questions
- Questions that establish mood and feeling
- Questions that foster beliefs and values
- Questions that foster insight

## ACTIVITIES FOR INTRODUCING REFLECTIVE THINKING TO PRACTITIONERS

The following activities will assist the facilitator of reflective practitioners with introducing reflective thinking. Activities involve formulating a definition of reflective thinking and using the reflective thinking model to enhance reflective thinking on the part of practitioners. By analyzing the model and illustrating the use of the process, practitioners should correlate the benefits of being reflective with problems in their own lives.

The first meeting with practitioners should be for the purpose of reviewing the model, as it is the central element of most of the tasks in this chapter. Activities are set up to facilitate ease of use. A topic and objective are provided along with a materials list and time constraints. The procedure for each task is systematically simple. Little preparation is needed after material gathering and reading for background knowledge has been completed. A description of several techniques used in the procedure section of each activity is found on previous pages in this chapter. Evaluations support the task objective. Debriefing questions are questions that should promote reflective thinking of practitioners at the conclusion of the activity, generally in a whole-group situation.

## *Task 1*    **Finding a Definition**

*Topic:* Defining Reflective Thinking

*Objective:* Participants will devise and revise a definition for reflective thinking by writing an initial definition, sharing it first with a colleague, then with the group, and finally reaching a consensus on one definition.

*Materials:* Chart paper or newsprint; masking tape; Post-it notes; Prominent Reflective Thinking Definitions (Table 1.4); Consensus Guidelines (Table 1.3)

*Time:* 30 minutes

*Procedure:*
1. Inform practitioners that to assess growth in reflective thinking, it is necessary to reach consensus on a definition. Distribute and review Consensus Guidelines.

2. Invite practitioners to write individual definitions of reflective thinking. Allow approximately 5 minutes.

3. Pair practitioners by allowing them to choose a peer with whom they have a high comfort level. Between the two, consensus must be reached and a second definition written on chart paper. Each pair should have the second definition written and displayed in a visible location and be prepared to discuss within 5 minutes.

4. Distribute one Post-it note to each practitioner. Instruct practitioners to vote by placing their Post-it note on the definition that most reflects their own thinking.

5. Discuss as a whole group why the majority definition was selected.

6. Distribute Prominent Reflective Thinking Definitions to practitioners. Compare the group definition with researched definitions.

*Evaluation:* Participants' definition had three commonalities found in most expert definitions: methodical process, inquiry orientation, and change or self-improvement as a goal.

*Debriefing:*
1. Was the individual definition easy to write? What made it easy? Difficult?

2. How were the paired partners able to reach consensus on a definition?

3. For what reason did you vote for a particular definition?

4. Why is it important to create a definition indicative of the practitioner?

5. How did the group's definition compare to the experts' definitions?

6. Were there commonalities among all definitions?

**Table 1.4**     Prominent Reflective Thinking Definitions

| | |
|---|---|
| Bigge and Shermis (1992) | Reflective learning is problem raising and problem solving. Fact-gathering is combined with deductive processes to construct, elaborate and test hypothesis. |
| Brubacher, Case, and Reagan (1994, p. 36) | [Reflective thinking is] our attempts to understand and make sense of the world. |
| Dewey (1933, p. 9) | [Reflective thinking is] active, persistent, and careful consideration of a belief or supposed form of knowledge in the light of the grounds that support it and the further conclusions to which it tends. |
| Lasley (1992, p. 24) | Reflection . . . refers to the capacity of a teacher to think creatively, imaginatively and at times, self-critically about classroom practice. |
| Norton (1994, p. 139) | [Reflective thinking is] a disciplined inquiry into the motives, methods, materials and consequences of educational practice. It enables practitioners to thoughtfully examine conditions and attitudes which impede or enhance student achievement. |
| Ross (1989, p. 22) | [Reflective thinking is] a way of thinking about educational matters that involves the ability to make rational choices and to assume responsibility for those choices. |
| Ross and Hannay (1986) | [Reflective thinking is] a process involving decision-making in a socio-political context, identification of problems, a search for satisfactory answers, and investigation of social problems realized in living. |
| Schön (1983, p. 151) | It [the cycle of inquiry] is initiated by the perception of something troubling or promising, and it is determined by the production of changes one finds on the whole satisfactory or by the discovery of new features which give the situation new meaning and change the nature of questions to be explored. |

Copyright © 2005 by Corwin Press. All rights reserved. Reprinted from *Promoting Reflective Thinking in Teachers: 50 Action Strategies* by Germaine Taggart and Alfred P. Wilson. Thousand Oaks, CA: Corwin Press, www.corwinpress.com. Reproduction authorized only for the local school site or nonprofit organization that has purchased the book.

### *Task 2*  The Reflective Thinking Process

*Topic:*  The Reflective Thinking Model

*Objective:*  The practitioner will review the Reflective Thinking Model, then present a scenario showing the components of the model through role-playing.

*Materials:*  Overhead transparency of Reflective Thinking Model (Figure 1.2); "Can't Sit Still" Scenario (Table 1.5), one copy for each participant—write or type on the bottom of each copy one of the following so that there is an even distribution of each: "Twinkle, Twinkle Little Star" "Row, Row, Row Your Boat" "Mary Had a Little Lamb" "Itsy, Bitsy Spider" "Old MacDonald"

*Time:*  1 hour

*Procedure:*  1. Present the model of reflective thinking to practitioners by using the Reflective Thinking Model. Discuss the cyclical nature of the model using the background information presented earlier in this chapter.

2. Distribute "Can't Sit Still" scenarios to practitioners. Have them read the scenarios silently. Discuss the facts within the scenario as they relate to the reflective thinking model.

| | |
|---|---|
| Problem: | Danny's excessive movement |
| Frame-reframe: | Arthritis causes need for movement |
| Possible solution | |
|    sets or intervention: | Cardboard office |
| Experimentation: | Use of cardboard office |
| Evaluation: | To be decided |
| Acceptance or rejection: | To be decided |

3. Group participants into five teams by referring them to the bottom of the scenario sheets, where you have written one of the earlier-mentioned children's song titles. Practitioners are to hum the tune of the song assigned to each of them as they navigate about the room listening for others humming the same tune. The last individual to enter the team is the leader.

4. Practitioners are to create a brief scenario to role-play for the whole group that depicts the reflective thinking model. Review role-playing rules. Allow 15 minutes for preparation.

5. Each team will present its role-play to the whole group. Immediately after each presentation, hold a brief discussion of the model components relative to the role-playing scenario. The overhead transparency of the model may be helpful in discussing the components.

*Evaluation:*  Scenarios used in role-play reflected components of the reflective thinking model.

*Debriefing:*  1. Does the model fully represent the process of reflective thinking?

2. Is one component more important than another?

3. Can you think of other scenarios that follow the reflective thinking model? Explain.

4. How might this model relate to journaling situations?

**Table 1.5**    "Can't Sit Still" Scenario

For the fourth time that morning, Danny had to be told to return to his seat, and once again, he returned to what he had been doing within a few minutes. His morning was spent dancing with the full-sized skeleton, looking out the window, picking on other students, and lying on the floor or his desk. "If I have to warn you again," said the teacher," you will visit the principal to discuss your problem!"

"But I wasn't doing anything!" Danny shouted, as he threw his pencil into the air.

"Write your name in the book," demanded the teacher.

Danny had been having problems all year. Because Danny has arthritis, he has two desks, which allows him to move from desk to desk whenever he feels the need. The problem is that he takes this privilege too far.

Danny has never been tested for a learning disability. He does attend a special reading class once a day. The remainder of his day is spent in the regular classroom.

"Today, we are going to try something different," the teacher said, as she walked to the back of the room. "I have an office that I want you to try." She set a large cardboard partition on Danny's desk. "Let's see if this helps you stay on task," she added.

Danny's mother is aware of Danny's problems at school. She visits with the teacher at least once a week. Danny also is required to take home daily assignment sheets. If there is a stamp on the sheet, Danny had a good day. Danny has a deal with his mother. If he brings home a certain number of good slips, she will take him to a basketball game.

Copyright © 2005 by Corwin Press. All rights reserved. Reprinted from *Promoting Reflective Thinking in Teachers: 50 Action Strategies* by Germaine Taggart and Alfred P. Wilson. Thousand Oaks, CA: Corwin Press, www.corwinpress.com. Reproduction authorized only for the local school site or nonprofit organization that has purchased this book.

## Task 3    Gardening Puzzle

*Topic:* Introduction of the Reflective Thinking Model

*Objective:* The practitioner will use the Reflective Thinking Model to devise a plan for partitioning a garden plot equitably among four individuals.

*Materials:* Reflective Thinking Model (Figure 1.2); copies of the Garden Plot Problem (Figure 1.3); Garden Plot Solution (Figure 1.4); colored pencils

*Time:* 20 minutes

*Procedure:* 1. Prior to the beginning of the session, use colored pencils to outline the garden plot on Garden Plot Problem copies. Use one color on two sheets, then a second on the next two sheets, and so on until all garden plots are color coded.

2. Group participants into pairs by the color coding on each person's Garden Plot Problem sheet.

3. Once participants are paired, allow 10 minutes for participants to process through the reflective thinking model to find a plausible solution to the following problem:

Four friends have recently purchased a garden plot in the shape shown. They want to divide it into four individual gardens that are the same shape and size. Help them solve their dilemma.

4. Call on a practitioner to demonstrate the solution on the overhead projector. Using the Garden Plot Solution, discuss the model and solutions.

*Evaluation:* Check for reasonable solutions that fit the criteria.

*Debriefing:* 1. Did the reflective thinking model provide a process for problem resolution?

2. Was reframing necessary?

3. What did each participant bring to the problem?

**Figure 1.3** Garden Plot Problem

Four friends have recently purchased a garden plot in the shape shown. They want to divide it into four individual gardens the same shape and size. Help them solve their dilemma.

Copyright © 2005 by Corwin Press. All rights reserved. Reprinted from *Promoting Reflective Thinking in Teachers: 50 Action Strategies*, by Germaine L. Taggart and Alfred P. Wilson. Thousand Oaks, CA: Corwin Press, www.corwinpress.com. Reproduction authorized only for the local school site or nonprofit organization that has purchased this book.

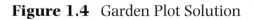

**Figure 1.4** Garden Plot Solution

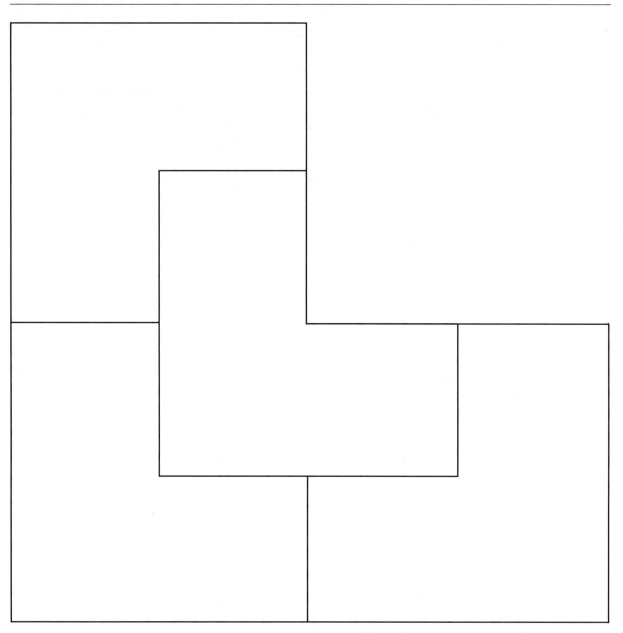

Copyright © 2005 by Corwin Press. All rights reserved. Reprinted from *Promoting Reflective Thinking in Teachers: 50 Action Strategies*, by Germaine L. Taggart and Alfred P. Wilson. Thousand Oaks, CA: Corwin Press, www.corwinpress.com. Reproduction authorized only for the local school site or nonprofit organization that has purchased this book.

## *Task 4*  **Roll On**

*Topic:* Introduction of the Reflective Thinking Model

*Objective:* The practitioner will use the Reflective Thinking Model to demonstrate the process of reflective thinking by devising possible solutions to the "roll on" dilemma.

*Materials:* Reflective Thinking Model (Figure 1.2); toilet paper rolls (enough for every team of three to have a unique design or color); Consensus Guidelines (Table 1.3)

*Time:* 20 minutes

*Procedure:* 1. Group participants by randomly distributing individual sections of various designs or colors of toilet paper.

2. Provide each team with a roll of toilet paper, and pose the following problem:

   Some individuals place toilet paper on the roller so that the end of the roll comes over the top toward the front; others prefer the end to dangle from the bottom at the back of the roll. If you want the end sheet to be at its most accessible point, what is your group's preference for placement of the roll on the toilet paper roller? Justify your answer.

3. Once participants are grouped, allow 10 minutes for participants to process through the reflective thinking model and reach consensus, then clarify and justify the team's position.

4. Randomly call team leaders (e.g., shortest person on each team) to explain the team's position.

*Evaluation:* Check for reasonableness of solutions and justifications.

*Debriefing:* 1. Consensus is an agreement by all participants on an issue. How was your team able to reach consensus?

2. Did the reflective thinking model provide a process for problem resolution?

3. Was reframing necessary?

4. What type of experimentation was necessary?

## Task 5    Designing a Classroom

*Topic:* Introduction of the Reflective Thinking Model

*Objective:* The practitioners will use the Reflective Thinking Model to devise a physical plan of a classroom housing 40 students that would accommodate team teaching by two teachers.

*Materials:* A deck of playing cards; Reflective Thinking Model (Figure 1.2); Classroom Layout (Figures 1.5A and 1.5B); Consensus Guidelines (Table 1.3)

*Time:* 40 minutes

*Procedure:* 1. Group participants in fours by randomly distributing playing cards (an ace, king, queen, jack, etc.) to each participant.

2. Provide each team with a copy of the Classroom Layout and present the following problem and scenario:

Devise a physical plan of a classroom housing 40 students that would accommodate team teaching by two teachers.

Scale is 1 cm = 4 ft. Each student desk is 2 ft long and 1½ ft wide. Teacher desks are 4 ft × 2 ft. Room size and layout are indicated on Classroom Layout sheets.

3. Once participants are grouped, allow 20 minutes for participants to process through the reflective thinking model, reach consensus on a layout, sketch it onto the grid paper, and develop justification for the solution.

4. Randomly call on a team leader (e.g., the person who has attended college the longest period of time) to present layout and justification.

*Evaluation:* Check for reasonableness of solutions and justification.

*Debriefing:* 1. Consensus is agreement by all participants on an issue. How was your team able to reach consensus?

2. Did the reflective thinking model provide a process for problem resolution?

3. What experiences were brought into the discussion?

4. How did the team evaluate the solution?

**Figure 1.5A**   Classroom Layout

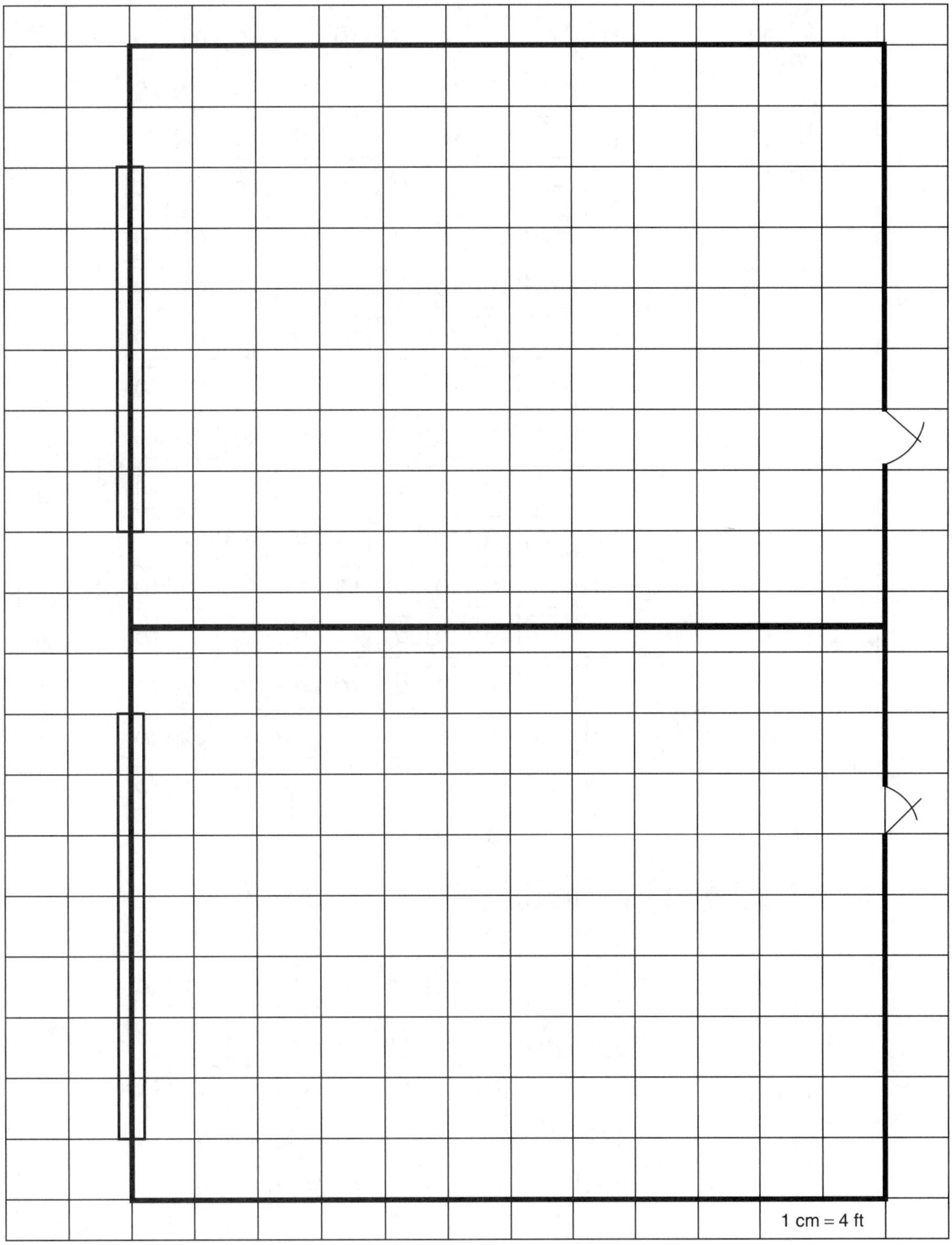

1 cm = 4 ft

Copyright © 2005 by Corwin Press. All rights reserved. Reprinted from *Promoting Reflective Thinking in Teachers: 50 Action Strategies*, by Germaine L. Taggart and Alfred P. Wilson. Thousand Oaks, CA: Corwin Press, www.corwinpress.com. Reproduction authorized only for the local school site or nonprofit organization that has purchased this book.

**26**

**Figure 1.5B** Classroom Furniture

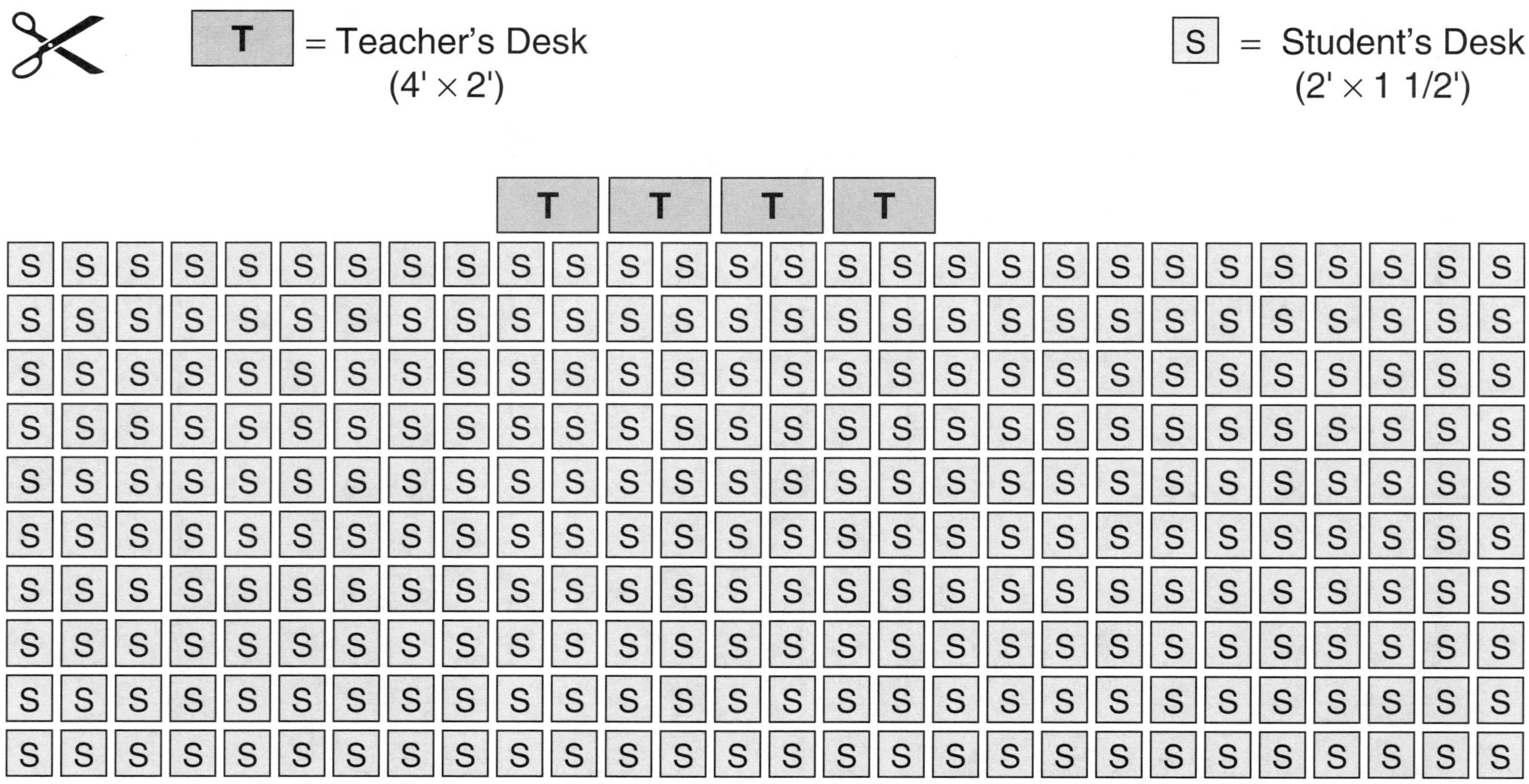

✂

| T | = Teacher's Desk (4' × 2') |

| S | = Student's Desk (2' × 1 1/2') |

NOTE: 1 cm = 4 ft

Copyright © 2005 by Corwin Press. All rights reserved. Reprinted from *Promoting Reflective Thinking in Teachers: 50 Action Strategies*, by Germaine L. Taggart and Alfred P. Wilson. Thousand Oaks, CA: Corwin Press, www.corwinpress.com. Reproduction authorized only for the local school site or nonprofit organization that has purchased this book.

## Task 6    Logic Lure

*Topic:* Introduction of the Reflective Thinking Model

*Objective:* The practitioner will use the Reflective Thinking Model to devise a plan for getting all characters in the dilemma to the opposite side of the river.

*Materials:* Reflective Thinking Model (Figure 1.2); Logic Lure (Figures) transparency (Figure 1.6—characters should be shaded or colored and cut out to allow for mobility when demonstrating the process); Logic Lure (Scene) (Figure 1.7)

*Time:* 20 minutes

*Procedure:* 1. Group participants into pairs, counting off by the number that when multiplied by two will equal the number of total practitioners.

2. Once practitioners are grouped, allow 10 minutes for them to process through the reflective thinking model to find a plausible solution to the problem that follows:

A boy owned a dog, a rabbit, and a bag of vegetables. One day, he was on the edge of a gorge, where there was a shaky old swinging bridge that was only strong and wide enough to hold him and one of his possessions. If he left the dog and rabbit alone, the dog would eat the rabbit. If he left the rabbit and the vegetables alone, the rabbit would eat the vegetables. How did he get safely across the gorge with all three of his possessions?

*Evaluation:* Check for reasonable solutions that fit the criteria.

*Debriefing:* 1. Did the reflective thinking model provide a process for problem resolution?

2. Was reframing necessary?

3. What did each participant bring to the problem?

**Figure 1.6** Logic Lure (Figures)

Maridith Bouchey 2/98

SOURCE: Maridith Bouchey. Used with permission.

**Figure 1.7** Logic Lure (Scene)

**Dog, Rabbit, and a Bag of Vegetables**

A boy owned a dog, a rabbit and a bag of vegetables. One day he was on the edge of a gorge, where there was a shaky old swinging bridge that was only strong and wide enough to hold him and one of his possessions. If he left the dog and rabbit alone, the dog would eat the rabbit. If he left the rabbit and the vegetables alone, the rabbit would eat the vegetables. How did he get safely across the gorge with all three of his possessions.

SOURCE: Maridith Bouchey. Used with permission.

# PREPARING A PLAN OF ACTION
# FOR ENHANCING REFLECTIVE THINKING

In discussing enhancing reflective thinking on the part of practitioners, Dewey (1933) recommends three attitudes that must be nurtured: open-mindedness, wholeheartedness, and intellectual responsibility. Open-mindedness refers to an intellectual receptiveness to alternatives. Wholeheartedness requires a mental, emotional, and physical commitment on the part of practitioners to solve problems. Reflective practitioners then consider intellectual responsibility toward long-term and short-term solutions to the problem.

Development of a plan to evaluate change is the final step toward enhancement of reflective thinking. The purpose of this step is threefold. First, practitioners examine the degree to which their plan is workable, given the constraints of the field setting and the degree to which those constraints can be overcome or can preclude the intervention's implementation. Second, there must be systematic monitoring of adherence to the plan. Self-evaluating and self-monitoring encourage and reinforce reflection on changes in teaching performance. Last, practitioners develop an evaluation plan to determine the effectiveness of the change. The facilitator provides a foundation and encourages practitioners to implement and follow the planning strategy and models, planning for evaluation as needed.

If the plan of action is successful, the practitioner has created a new understanding and reached a higher level of reflection. If the plan of action is unsuccessful, the practitioner continues the cycle of inquiry and reflection, taking into consideration the new information resulting from unsuccessful experimentation toward reaching a goal. Thus, the cycle parallels the reflective thinking model.

During a final 1-hour or 2-hour experience, whether it be in short sessions with preservice practitioners or at the end of a seminar experience, allow practitioners time to develop a plan of action for future growth in reflective thinking. Practitioners will develop one or two specific goals. For each goal, a list of strategies will be made that support reaching the goal. Strategies may include those incorporated throughout the guide, or practitioners may want to select particular strategies indicative of a focus area of concern. Each strategy should be outlined in terms of tasks for completion; target completion dates; and necessary materials, input, and knowledge to complete the task.

Monitoring of the goal's achievement should be formative as well as summative. Identifying those constraints that may serve to block achievement of the goal is essential. Identification of those support resources that will serve to augment goal achievement is equally essential. Devise a monitoring strategy. Establish how feedback will be collected and evaluated. Also, establish definitive criteria for determining that a goal has been met. Most important, plan for success, and plan to celebrate success. Communicate to others your achievements. Tables 1.6 and 1.7 may be used to provide a basic structure with which to create a plan to enhance reflective thinking.

**Table 1.6**     Preparing a Plan of Action

- Strategy

- Tasks for completion

- Target completion date

- Necessary materials

- Input

- Knowledge needed to complete the task

- Monetary considerations

- Constraints

- Suggested resources

- Collection of information and feedback

- Evaluation and feedback

Copyright © 2005 by Corwin Press. All rights reserved. Reprinted from *Promoting Reflective Thinking in Teachers: 50 Action Strategies*, by Germaine L. Taggart and Alfred P. Wilson. Thousand Oaks, CA: Corwin Press, www.corwinpress.com. Reproduction authorized only for the local school site or nonprofit organization that has purchased this book.

**Table 1.7**  Plan of Action: Enhancement of Reflective Thinking

**Goal**

| Strategy | Tasks | Completion Date | Support Materials | Constraints | Monitoring Method and Criteria | Method of Calibration |
|---|---|---|---|---|---|---|
| | | | | | | |
| | | | | | | |

Copyright © 2005 by Corwin Press. All rights reserved. Reprinted from *Promoting Reflective Thinking in Teachers: 50 Action Strategies* by Germaine Taggart and Alfred P. Wilson. Thousand Oaks, CA: Corwin Press, www.corwinpress.com. Reproduction authorized only for the local school site or nonprofit organization that has purchased this book.

# 2

# Assessing Reflective Thinking

*It is more important to make teachers thoughtful and alert students of education than it is to help them get immediate proficiency.*

—Dewey (1933)

---

### *Chapter Objectives*

**The facilitator will**

- Determine a baseline level of reflection
- Assess personal and practitioner growth in reflective thinking
- Understand the attributes that are indicative of reflective practitioners
- Determine a level of reflection in writing

---

The benefits of reflective thinking are great. But how do you know where an individual functions as a reflective practitioner? How can you establish a baseline so that growth in reflection can be assessed? What constitutes evidence of reflection?

Little has been done to systematically assess reflective thinking. In fact, some proponents of reflective thinking contend that assessment in any quantifiable form is invalid (Ross, 1990), because the reflective thinking process cannot be observed and because agreement on a definition of reflective thinking has not yet been ascertained (Hattan & Smith, 1994). Zeichner and Liston (1987) followed preservice teachers into their professional careers to continue monitoring reflective growth. Kirby and Teddlie (1989) and Cruickshank

(1985) also measured reflective thinking of practitioners at a technical level. Program effectiveness was studied by Korthagen (1985); Korthagen and Wubbels (1991); Ross (1989); and Sparks-Langer, Colton, Pasch, and Starko (1991). Little can be generalized from these evaluation attempts because the "means for gathering and analyzing data pose a considerable challenge for researchers, for it is difficult to establish unequivocally that reflection has taken place" (Hattan & Smith, 1994, p. 5).

Evaluative efforts have often been qualitative in nature, studying the impact of reflective thinking at the preservice level. Qualitative research allows the researcher to view development of reflection in context. The use of preservice teachers provides a manageable population in size and setting. Such studies provide only isolated reports of program success or growth in reflective levels (Cole & Knowles, 2000; Conway, 2001; Tillema, 2000; Tillema & Kremer-Hayon, 2002; Zeichner, 1987).

Several teacher educators have researched ways to analyze and code writing samples of practitioners (Hattan & Smith, 1995; Ross, 1990; Simmons & Sparks, 1987). Written assignments, such as journaling, autobiographical sketches, and narratives, are ways of recording reflective thoughts. Concerns were voiced, however, as to the ability of those thoughts to be translated into reflective action.

Sparks-Langer et al. (1991) provide three orientations to reflective thinking of practitioners: cognitive, critical, and narrative. The cognitive approach emphasizes decision making based on information gathering and processing. The critical approach focuses on problem framing using ethical and moral reasoning. Teacher experiences, values, sociopolitical implications, and goals form the benchmarks for decision making. The narrative approach uses personal narratives, naturalistic inquiry, case studies, and action research to focus on circumstances under which decision making takes place.

Eastern Michigan University was the setting for Sparks-Langer et al.'s (1991) studies on reflective thinking of preservice teachers. A framework (see Table 2.1) for measuring and describing reflective thinking types was developed to show "a growing sophistication of teachers' schemata . . . from technical concepts and rules to contextual and ethical thinking" (p. 7). The framework shows seven levels of reflection. The first level indicates no descriptive language, and the second suggests a simple layperson's description. Little, if any, reflection takes place at these two levels. At levels three and four, events labeled with appropriate terms and explanation, with tradition or personal preference given as the rationale, respectively, are indicative of the technical mode of reflective thinking. Levels five and six consist of explanation with principle or theory given as the rationale, and explanation with principle or theory and consideration of context factors, respectively, which are indicative of practitioners functioning at a contextual level. Level seven presents explanations that consider ethical, moral, and political issues, which are characteristics of practitioners functioning at the dialectical level.

**Table 2.1**    Framework for Reflective Thinking

| Level | Description |
| --- | --- |
| 1 | No descriptive language |
| 2 | Simple, layperson description |
| 3 | Events labeled with appropriate terms |
| 4 | Explanation with tradition or personal preference given as the rationale |
| 5 | Explanation with principle or theory given as the rationale |
| 6 | Explanation with principle or theory and consideration of context factors |
| 7 | Explanation with consideration of ethical, moral, and political issues |

SOURCE: Sparks-Langer et al. (1991, p. 26). Reprinted with permission.

Hattan and Smith (1995) assessed the reflective process in an attempt to identify evidence of reflection by focusing on defining characteristics of individuals' writing. Four writing styles and defining criteria were developed and tested. The first, *descriptive writing,* was not considered reflective as only a description was present with no attempt made to provide rationale or take issue with an event. The second writing style was termed *descriptive reflection.* Criteria included justification in addition to description, often based on experience. The third writing style, labeled *dialogic reflection,* was written in third person with judgments, exploration of reasoning, and recognition of multiple perspectives. *Critical reflection,* the fourth writing style, has the individual responding to episodes by relating to influences of multiple historical and sociopolitical contexts.

In looking for other criteria for assessment of reflective thinking, Noordhoff and Kleinfeld (1990) looked at videotaping episodes followed by conferencing with practitioners as a way to reflect on teaching purpose and methodology. Though time-consuming and, at the preservice level, often contrived, Noordhoff and Kleinfeld contend that teaching behavior and judgment can be assessed using videotape. Their experience in rural Alaska shows that preservice teachers, through microteaching assessments, could move from viewing teaching as task oriented to viewing the teaching experience as a problematic act dependent on contextual factors—indicating growth from the technical level of reflection to the contextual level. Rubric construction provides a way to analyze effective teaching. Narratives reflecting on the microteaching experience and evaluated using criteria from the Reflective Thinking Pyramid (see Figure 1.1) provide a means for determining level of reflection for teaching actions.

The Reflective Thinking Pyramid, by definition, builds progressively from a basic general premise to a peak of reflection epitomized by individual autonomy and self-understanding. The base of the pyramid is a technical level where knowledge is derived from human experience as well as pedagogy, content, and methodology of education. Practitioners bring to the educational experience past histories and knowledge gleaned from content, skills, and behavior observations to produce reflective individuals capable of meeting set outcomes; learning theory to support a skill base; and making simple, rational observations. The technical level is evidenced in the writing of practitioners who

- Make simple descriptions of observations
- Focus on behaviors, content, and skills from past experiences or theory derived from readings or course work, without looking for alternatives
- Are task oriented, viewing teaching competency as meeting a set of objectives
- Use appropriate educational vocabulary to correspond with the current skill and pedagogy level

Practitioners reflecting at the contextual level of the pyramid have progressed to a comfort level evidenced by a willingness to look for alternative approaches that best fit the needs of the students and the context of the situation—choices based on knowledge and value commitments and analysis, clarification, and validation of principles found in teaching. The contextual level is evidenced in the writing of practitioners who

- Reflect on practices as they affect students' learning
- Reflect on decisions relative to the context of the situation
- Relate theory to practice
- Focus on action
- Look for alternatives to practice based on knowledge and personal values
- Analyze, clarify, and validate practices based on sound teaching constructs

Practitioners reflecting at the dialectical level of the pyramid have progressed to an autonomous state evidenced by disciplined inquiry, reflection-in-action, self-actualization, and an open-mindedness that allow them to address moral, ethical, and sociopolitical issues in teaching. The dialectical level is evidenced in the writing of practitioners who

- Systematically question practices
- Suggest alternatives and competing theories
- Reflect on decisions and consequences during the course of the action
- Bring moral, ethical, and sociopolitical issues to bear on educational practices
- Express themselves verbally and in their writing with efficacy and self-confidence

Several researchers have explored the correlation among reflective thinking and various attributes associated with effective practitioners. LaBoskey's study (as cited in Copeland, Birmingham, De La Cruz, & Lewin, 1993) investigated a connection between reflectivity and a proactive nature. Zeichner and Liston (1987) suggested that teachers' value systems are related to reflectivity. Wubbels and Korthagen (1990) indicated that reflective teachers are open to innovation and that relationships with students and colleagues are more favorable with higher levels of reflective thinking. Improvement in teaching (Bolin, 1988; Munby & Russell, 1989) and heightened connections between theory and practice were evident in reflective educators (Cruickshank, 1985). Giovannelli (2003) examined how variations in reflective disposition toward teaching influence effective teaching.

A collective list of practitioner attributes (see Table 2.2) from the research, which are believed to be evidence of reflective thinking, provides a core for the Profile of Reflective Thinking Attributes (see Form 2.1). The profile, not meant to be a quantitative diagnostic tool of reflective thinking in and of itself, should be given to practitioners at the onset of sessions on reflective thinking. There are no right or wrong answers. No stigma should be placed on the practitioner's identification within any level. The instrument is designed to be one of several tools used in triangulation of data to assess an approximate baseline level of reflection so that growth may be determined. "Triangulation is the act of bringing more than one source of data to bear on a single point" (Marshall & Rossman, 1995, p. 144). Data from a variety of sources corroborate and elaborate upon the findings. Analogous to this concept are the quantitative tools, such as blood pressure instruments or thermometers, with which a physician collects information to get a more holistic picture of the health of a patient.

**Table 2.2**    Reflective Thinking Attributes

*Reflective practitioners . . .*

Identify and analyze problems and situations

Look at problems relative to educational, social, and ethical issues

Critically consider contextual and pedagogical factors

Use a rational problem-solving approach

Make intuitive, creative interpretations and judgments

Are metacognitively, analytically, and instructionally skillful

Possess self-efficacy, intrinsic motivation, and a desire for lifelong learning

Are open to experimentation and new innovations

Experience job satisfaction

Make decisions consciously and carefully

View situations from multiple perspectives

Set personal short-term and long-term goals

Plan and monitor actions, then evaluate results of those actions

Have essential skills for attaining and using information

Correct understandings of underlying facts, procedures, and skills

Consider general characteristics of so-called best practice

Are flexible in a search for alternative explanations

Use evidence in supporting or evaluating a decision or position

Have a commitment to values (e.g., all students can learn)

Have a strong commitment to systematic and rational reflective thinking

Show responsiveness to educational needs of students

Question personal aims and actions

Constantly review instructional goals, methods, and materials

Are a proactive force in education

Are intellectually perceptive to multiple and novel ideas

Are committed to problem resolution (wholeheartedness)

Commit adequate resources to reflective thinking (time as well as physical, mental, and emotional energy)

Welcome peer review, critique, and advice

Write (journal) events reflectively

SOURCE: Adapted from Dewey (1933); LaBoskey as cited in Copeland, Birmingham, De La Cruz, and Lewin (1993); Ross (1989); Schön (1987); Simmons and Sparks (1987); Sparks-Langer et al. (1991).

**Form 2.1**    Profile of Reflective Thinking Attributes

To explore your current level of reflective thinking, respond to the following questions. For each statement, circle the number of the indicator that best reflects your agreement:

4 = Almost always
3 = On a regular basis
2 = Situational
1 = Seldom

**When confronted with a problem situation,**

| | | | | | |
|---|---|---|---|---|---|
| 1. | I can identify a problem situation | 4 | 3 | 2 | 1 |
| 2. | I analyze a problem based upon the needs of the student | 4 | 3 | 2 | 1 |
| 3. | I seek evidence that supports or refutes my decision | 4 | 3 | 2 | 1 |
| 4. | I view the problem situation in an ethical context | 4 | 3 | 2 | 1 |
| 5. | I use an organized approach to problem solving | 4 | 3 | 2 | 1 |
| 6. | I am intuitive in making judgments | 4 | 3 | 2 | 1 |
| 7. | I creatively interpret the situation | 4 | 3 | 2 | 1 |
| 8. | My actions vary with the context of the situation | 4 | 3 | 2 | 1 |
| 9. | I feel most comfortable with a set routine | 4 | 3 | 2 | 1 |
| 10. | I have strong commitment to values (e.g., all students can learn) | 4 | 3 | 2 | 1 |
| 11. | I am responsive to the educational needs of students | 4 | 3 | 2 | 1 |
| 12. | I review my personal aims and actions | 4 | 3 | 2 | 1 |
| 13. | I am flexible in my thinking | 4 | 3 | 2 | 1 |
| 14. | I have a questioning nature | 4 | 3 | 2 | 1 |
| 15. | I welcome peer review of my actions | 4 | 3 | 2 | 1 |

*(Continued)*

**Form 2.1** (Continued)

**When preparing, implementing, and assessing a lesson,**

| | | | | | |
|---|---|---|---|---|---|
| 16. | Innovative ideas are often used | 4 | 3 | 2 | 1 |
| 17. | My focus is on the objective of each lesson | 4 | 3 | 2 | 1 |
| 18. | I feel there is no one best approach to teaching | 4 | 3 | 2 | 1 |
| 19. | I have the skills necessary to be a successful teacher | 4 | 3 | 2 | 1 |
| 20. | I have the knowledge necessary to be a successful teacher | 4 | 3 | 2 | 1 |
| 21. | I consciously modify my teaching to meet student needs | 4 | 3 | 2 | 1 |
| 22. | I complete tasks adequately | 4 | 3 | 2 | 1 |
| 23. | I understand concepts, underlying facts, procedures, and skills | 4 | 3 | 2 | 1 |
| 24. | I consider the social implications of so-called best practice | 4 | 3 | 2 | 1 |
| 25. | I set long-term goals | 4 | 3 | 2 | 1 |
| 26. | I self-monitor my actions | 4 | 3 | 2 | 1 |
| 27. | I evaluate my teaching effectiveness | 4 | 3 | 2 | 1 |
| 28. | My students meet my instructional objective when evaluated | 4 | 3 | 2 | 1 |
| 29. | I use a journal regularly | 4 | 3 | 2 | 1 |
| 30. | I engage in action research | 4 | 3 | 2 | 1 |

Tally how many times you circled each indicator, write the number of each tally below, multiply by the indicator number, then add the subtotals to reach an overall score.

Indicator 4 × _____ = _____

Indicator 3 × _____ = _____

Indicator 2 × _____ = _____

Indicator 1 × _____ = _____

Total = _____

Copyright © 1996 by G. Taggart.

Practitioners mark the Profile of Reflective Thinking Attributes instrument, tally the number of circled indicators, place the numbers on the line after the appropriate indicator on the second page, then multiply the indicator by the tally number to arrive at a subtotal. Practitioners then add the four subtotals together and write the score in the space indicated. Use the following scale of totals to determine the appropriate level of reflection.

Technical level = Below 75
Contextual level = 75 to 104
Dialectical level = 104 to 120

Provide for discussion following the use of this instrument. Here are some possible debriefing questions:

- What level(s) of reflection was (were) most evident? Why do you suppose this level was most prevalent?
- Which of the attributes do you consider to be the most indicative of a reflective practitioner?
- How might the information gleaned from completing this profile help you in achieving growth of reflective thinking?

Using the "Attribute Clarification" or "Card Sort: Reflective Thinking Attributes" activities in this chapter will support the use of the Profile of Reflective Thinking Attributes and assist practitioners in defining a reflective practitioner. Stress to practitioners that this is only one indication of a baseline level of reflection. There are no right or wrong answers. No stigma should be attached to reflection level.

The following activities may be used after practitioners have completed the Profile of Reflective Thinking Attributes. The activities are intended to validate the attributes found in the profile and clarify reflective thinking and levels of reflection.

## *Task 7*   Attribute Clarification

*Topic:* Attributes of reflective thinking practitioners

*Objective:* Practitioners will use the attributes found in the Profile of Reflective Thinking Attributes to create possible examples or actions derived from possession of the attributes.

*Materials:* Profile of Reflective Thinking Attributes (Form 2.1); three sheets of chart paper or newsprint placed about the room on which 10 profile statements have been written so that teams may write examples of each attribute under the corresponding attribute; watercolor markers

*Time:* 45 minutes

*Procedure:* 1. Allow 5 minutes for practitioners to respond to the Profile of Reflective Thinking Attributes. Collect responses.

2. Group practitioners into teams by age of students taught either in field experience or in their own classrooms. Be sure teams are manageable in size—split teams of more than five practitioners. Allow for no single-practitioner groups.

3. Instruct practitioners to review 10 of the items on the profile. Designate which 10 items (i.e., 1–10, 11–20, or 21–30) each team will discuss. This may be done arbitrarily, but work to be sure each set of items has an equal number of teams reviewing it. Teams are to briefly discuss each item, then create two or three possible examples or actions derived from possession of the attributes. Allow 10 minutes for discussion at the end of which practitioners will have written their examples, using the watercolor markers, under the appropriate profile item on the chart paper spaced around the room.

4. After the first set of 10 attributes is reviewed, move teams clockwise to the next set of 10 items. Allow 10 minutes for practitioners to add examples or actions to those on the chart. Move teams a third time and repeat the process with the last set of items.

5. Discuss the types of examples and actions that practitioners have determined are indicative of each attribute.

*Evaluation:* Practitioners collectively provided 8 to 10 examples or actions that are indicative of each attribute.

*Debriefing:* 1. Were there attributes that prompted a higher degree of knowledge? Experience?

2. Were there attributes that were found more readily in the actions of team members? Less readily?

3. Which attributes indicate a higher level of reflection on the part of the practitioner?

4. Are there attributes not on the list that you feel should be included?

## Task 8  Card Sort: Reflective Thinking Attributes

*Topic:* Attributes of reflective practitioners

*Objective:* Practitioners will analyze attributes indicative of reflective practitioners, then self-evaluate their possession of these attributes.

*Materials:* Profile of Reflective Thinking Attributes (Form 2.1); Attribute Cards (Table 2.3) xeroxed on six different colors of paper, then laminated and cut apart; Category Cards (Table 2.4) photocopied, laminated, and cut apart; overhead transparency of the Reflective Thinking Pyramid (Figure 1.1)

*Time:* 30 minutes

*Procedure:* 1. Allow 5 minutes for practitioners to respond to the Profile of Reflective Thinking Attributes. Collect responses.

2. Group practitioners by distributing one of each of the six colors of cards randomly to each participant so that six equal teams are formed. Give each team the remainder of the cards that match the color of the cards they were given (i.e., all green cards form a team, all reds form a team, etc.).

3. Explain to practitioners that the cards contain attributes of effective teaching. Participants are to sort cards into three categories. The first category, labeled *Technical*, will include those attributes that apply to practitioners who bring to the educational experience knowledge gleaned from content, skills, and behavior observations. Focus is on a competency level that allows practitioners to meet a set of predetermined objectives. A second category, labeled *Contextual*, will represent attributes of teachers who look for alternative approaches that best fit the needs of students and the context of the situation. A third category, *Dialectical*, will reflect cards dealing with attributes of teachers who function at a critical thinking level that addresses morals, values, and sociopolitical issues. Each attribute card can be placed in only one category or column. Allow 15 minutes for this exercise.

4. Instruct teams to discuss the rationale for placement of attribute cards into each category. Teams should also discuss individuals' self-evaluation of possession of these attributes.

5. Discuss the Reflective Thinking Pyramid and its use in assessing reflection.

*Evaluation:* Practitioners sorted attribute cards according to category, then self-evaluated possession of attributes.

*Debriefing:* 1. Are reflective practitioners effective practitioners? Provide rationale for your answer.

2. Could some of the attribute cards fit into other categories? Why do you think so?

3. Where do you believe reflection begins? How can you tell if you are reflective?

4. Was there a particular category in which most practitioners found themselves?

**Table 2.3**     Attribute Cards

| | |
|---|---|
| Identifies and analyzes problem-solving situations | Uses a rational problem approach |
| Looks at problems relative to educational, social, and ethical issues | Critically considers contextual and pedagogical factors |
| Makes creative interpretations and judgments | Experiences job satisfaction |
| Is metacognitively, analytically, and instructively intuitive | Views situations from multiple perspectives |
| Possesses self-efficacy, intrinsic motivation, and a desire for lifelong learning | Sets personal short-term and long-term goals |
| Is open to experimentation and new innovations | Makes decisions consciously and carefully |
| Plans, monitors, then evaluates actions | Searches for alternative results |
| Has essential skills for mastering concepts and using information | Corrects understandings of underlying facts, procedures, and skills |
| Considers general characteristics of so-called best practice | Questions personal aims and actions |

| | |
|---|---|
| Uses evidence in supporting or evaluating a decision or position | Has a commitment to values (e.g., all students can learn) |
| Has a strong commitment to systematic and rational reflective thinking | Is a proactive force in education |
| Shows responsiveness to educational and instructional needs of students | Constantly reviews goals, methods, and materials |
| Is intellectually receptive to multiple and novel ideas | Possesses flexibility in thinking |
| Is committed to problem resolution (wholeheartedness) | Writes (journals) events reflectively |
| Commits adequate resources to reflective thinking (time as well as mental, physical, and emotional energy) | Welcomes peer review, critique, and advice |
| Commits to reaching objectives | Implements discipline system |
| Is task oriented | Focuses on lesson design and implementation |

Copyright © 2005 by Corwin Press. All rights reserved. Reprinted from *Promoting Reflective Thinking in Teachers: 50 Action Strategies,* by Germaine L. Taggart and Alfred P. Wilson. Thousand Oaks, CA: Corwin Press, www.corwinpress.com. Reproduction authorized only for the local school site or nonprofit organization that has purchased this book.

**Table 2.4**    Category Cards

| | |
|---|---|
| Technical | Contextual |
| Dialectical | |

# 3

# Practicing Observational Learning

*Observational learning is theoretically conceptualized as a skill that can be developed along a learning hierarchy from acquisition and fluency to generalization of initiative behavior.*

—Browder, Schoen, and Lentz (1986–87, p. 447)

---

### Chapter Objectives

**The facilitator will**

- Assist practitioners in demonstrating proficiency in the use of the observational strategy
- Be able to assess growth in reflective thinking on application of the strategy
- Analyze personal competence of the strategy to assist practitioners in preparing action plans that will foster personal reflection on return to the classroom situation
- Facilitate maintenance of reflective journals to be used by practitioners for personal growth assessment and for peer assessment

---

Teacher educators who support the concept of reflective thinking use several strategies that provide input and modeling coupled with experiences to develop metacognitive skills. These skills and experiences may also enhance reflective thinking of practitioners (Bullough, 1991; Connelly & Clandinin, 1986; Hattan & Smith, 1995; Korthagen, 1985; Sparks-Langer et al., 1991). Among those strategies found to be most effective and functional with practitioners are observational learning; journaling; narratives; practicum techniques; mental processes, such as metaphors and repertory grids; community dialogue; and inquiry-oriented processes. Throughout the remainder of this book, these strategies will be discussed; uses at the technical, contextual, and dialectical levels will be provided; and follow-up activities will be suggested. Chapter 3 deals with the enhancement of observational skills to bring about growth in reflective thinking.

## THE OBSERVATION PROCESS

Bandura (1968) defines observational learning as one's ability to acquire new responses by observing the behavior of a model. Much of what is learned in education happens through observation. Observation is a skill that practitioners must possess to develop insights needed to make wise decisions. Observations should be ongoing, systematic, and developed to the point that a focus can be established, notes taken, and actions explored in a relatively short amount of time with high effectiveness. Inferences and judgments are not components of the observation process, which makes the observation skill difficult for many practitioners, especially novices. According to McHaney and Impey (1992), judgmental statements are generally nonspecific and undefined, whereas descriptive statements are specifically defined. Examples of these two types of statements follow.

Judgmental: The child responded well to questioning.

Descriptive: The child responded correctly to five out of six questions.

Techniques that facilitate observational skills in novice practitioners are the determination of a single focus, setting minimum time constraints and developing criteria and instrumentation to make collection of observational data easier to accomplish. As practitioners become more skilled, scripting in the form of narratives, anecdotal records, running records, and visual mapping may be possible, providing for thick descriptions similar to the information-laden documents of ethnographers. Narratives are open-ended, low-structured descriptions of events. Anecdotal records differ from narratives as a particular event is described with detail. Two parts of anecdotal records are facts and interpretations of facts. Running records are kept on the occurrences of an observational objective over a period of time and without judgment or interpretation. Visual mapping is a way of using images of an observation rather than words. Seating charts or drawings of room arrangements are forms of visual mapping.

Instruments of observation should be easy to use and readily adapted for a variety of purposes and time constraints. Rating scales (Borich, 1994, 2003) provide simple instruments for recording behavior as well as the degree to which behaviors occur. Examples are checklists and Likert scales. Checklists tend to be more subjective, whereas Likert scales are often objective, incorporating judgment and interpretation on the part of the observer. Other instruments may be designed to allow observers to tally occurrences of a particular event.

Experience with observational practice brings opportunity for more complex foci, longer time limits, and flexibility in criteria and instrumentation.

Possible foci for observations are

- Individual behaviors
- Lesson structure
- Attitudes toward technology
- Roles of teachers
- Classroom management effectiveness
- Teaching techniques
- Student response to teaching techniques
- Relationships between and among practitioners, students, and so on

Observations may be made as participant observers or nonparticipant observers. As participant observers, duties within the classroom are simultaneously carried out along with the observation process. Nonparticipant observers are looking in on the action, taking a third-person point of view. In either instance, the practitioner engages in attempts to understand perceptions through indicators such as overt behaviors, verbal expressions, or subtle body language.

Browder et al. (1986–87) suggest that observational skills are developed at three levels: *acquisition*, imitation of a discrete model; *fluency*, imitation of complex functional behaviors with greater independence; and *generalization*, imitation of behavior of a withdrawn model. This hierarchy can aid in determining level of observational skills, recognizing essential variables in planning, and organizing instruction that will enhance the practitioner's ability to acquire more complex behaviors.

According to Borich (1994, 2003), observation learning plans should be developed and revised for self-improvement at a level that matches one's own stage of experience. Borich also lists eight goals of observation:

1. To achieve empathy

2. To establish cooperative relationships

3. To become realistic

4. To establish direction

5. To attain confidence

6. To release enthusiasm

7. To become flexible

8. To become self-reliant

Systematic observational learning

- Encourages view of practitioner as a flexible decision maker
- Fosters realistic view of teaching as a profession
- Allows focus on specific skills
- Allows practitioners to relate better to students
- Fosters higher levels of comfort within the classroom for practitioners
- Allows practitioners time to view teaching behaviors modeled by others
- Permits practitioners to observe parallels of teaching behaviors and student learning behaviors
- Provides common vernacular
- Fosters self-improvement

Learning is not only dependent on what we see but also on how those observations are processed. Separating dialogue from observation is not conducive to developing shared understandings of educative practice (Clarke, 1995). Dialogue between and among practitioners and facilitators provides a forum for the sorting out of facts and interpretations and for working through the problem-solving process. Facts and interpretations may be looked at more critically. Multiple perspectives are brought to bear on the observational situation.

Debriefing questions built into the activities presented in this chapter are intended for use in a collaborative environment. The facilitator is to foster discussion of observation to analyze, clarify, and evaluate the learning environment. Subsequent discussion can be conducted through study groups or asynchronous electronic formats. Activities are written at each of the three reflective levels: technical, contextual, and dialectical. Activity selection should be based on the experiences of practitioners and levels of reflection determined by using the Profile of Reflective Thinking Attributes (see Form 2.1).

## REFLECTIVE ACTIVITIES

### Technical

At a technical level, practitioners generally have not had many experiences to help them formulate solutions to problematic classroom situations. The following two activities, "Categorization of Observations" (Task 9) and "Compliance With Classroom Rules" (Task 10), will assist practitioners in building nonjudgmental observations, creating simple instruments for recording observations, and interpreting data collected from observations.

*(Text continues on p. 68)*

## Task 9   Categorization of Observations

*Topic:* Observational learning

*Objective:* The practitioner will prepare a list of classroom observations, then categorize them according to "Roles in the Classroom," "Classroom Environment," "Communication," and "Professionalism."

*Materials:* Clear transparencies; markers; four newsprint charts placed about the room, labeled "Roles in the Classroom," "Classroom Environment," "Communication," and "Professionalism."

*Time:* 30 minutes

*Procedure:*  1. Instruct practitioners to individually observe the current classroom setting for 5 minutes, listing observations on a piece of notepaper. During the observation period, provide a variety of short activities for participants, such as discussing room arrangement, summarizing activities to this point in the session, asking for points of clarification from practitioners, and so on. As a facilitator, be mobile; vary your voice tone, volume, and inflection; use proximity; dress professionally; and use educational terminology.

2. Divide practitioners into groups of four or five based on shoe color. The individual on each team who drives the greatest distance to the session will be the leader. The individual who drives the shortest distance will be the recorder.

3. Teams are to collectively analyze the lists of each individual according to the following topics: "Roles in the Classroom", "Classroom Environment", "Communication", and "Professionalism". The observations are then to be placed on the corresponding topic sheet hanging about the room. If the item already appears on the newsprint list, there is no need to repeat it. Allow 15 minutes for discussion and transfer of lists by the recorders.

4. Select the leaders of four of the teams to each summarize one of the newsprint lists. Input derived from team discussion may be obtained from the leaders as well as members of the whole group. The aim is to discuss how each item, in turn, fits under one of the categories.

*Evaluation:* Practitioners observed the classroom setting, compiled a list of observations, and collectively categorized the observations.

*Debriefing:*  1. What other categories might be appropriate for placement of some of your observations?

2. Did any of your observations not fit in one of the categories? Were there observations that could fit in more than one category?

3. Did inferences enter into your observations? If so, what might be the effect of allowing inferences to alter actual observations?

4. What are other possible observational strategies for recording the information observed?

| **Task 10** | **Compliance With Classroom Rules** |

*Topic:* Observational learning

*Objective:* The practitioner will create an observation instrument, then use it while observing the current classroom environment and assessing the number of students who comply with all classroom rules throughout a preset 15-minute period.

*Materials:* Clear transparencies (two for facilitator and one for each team); transparency of the Observation Instrument (Table 3.1) and enough copies for teams of three participants

*Time:* Two 20-minute periods; one 15-minute classroom observation

*Procedure:* **Day 1**

1. Ask practitioners to briefly discuss possible classroom rules with an individual near them, then list them on a sheet of paper. Allow 5 minutes.

2. During whole-group discussion, reach consensus on four or five rules typically found in a classroom setting. Stress that rules are to be stated in a positive manner. Write the rules on a clear transparency placed on the overhead projector.

3. Discuss a possible format that would allow practitioners to reach the objective. Possible alternatives are tally sheets, rating scales, or checklists. Each would indicate the classroom rules and means for marking the observed behaviors. Show transparency of the Observation Instrument (Table 3.1). Add rules suggested by practitioners and possible adaptations to reach objectives.

4. Distribute individual copies of the Observation Instrument and assign a revision of the instrument to meet the needs of the practitioners. Practitioners may work in twos or threes based on grade or age level for classroom assignments. Fifteen minutes of observation are to be made in a current classroom environment. Practitioners are to record the number of students who comply with classroom rules throughout that time period using the instrument designed.

Note: Variations to the instrument may include
a. Separate columns for males and females
b. Specific area to record comments regarding actions of those who are not complying with rules
c. Simultaneous use of the instrument during the same classroom episode by two observers, with later comparisons made

**Day 2**

1. Practitioners will be teamed in the same groups formed to create the observation instrument. Each team will elect a leader. Allow 5 minutes for teams to collect thoughts on the value of the instrument created and used in recording desired data. Provide each team with a transparency on which to sketch the instrument.

2. Call on the leaders of each team in turn to briefly explain to the whole group their instrument and its value. Encourage practitioners to use the overhead and the sketch of the instrument to facilitate understanding of the team's efforts.

*Evaluation:* An instrument was created that focuses on observation of students complying with classroom rules

*Debriefing:* 1. What are suggested ways of adapting the instrument to meet the practitioners' needs?

2. Are other topics suitable for observations? What might they be?

3. Why is it important to record only observable behaviors?

4. At what point are practitioners' inferences justifiable?

5. How might data collected from an observation instrument be used?

**Table 3.1**     Observation Instrument

| *Classroom Rules* | |
|---|---|
| | |

Copyright © 2005 by Corwin Press. All rights reserved. Reprinted from *Promoting Reflective Thinking in Teachers: 50 Action Strategies*, by Germaine L. Taggart and Alfred P. Wilson. Thousand Oaks, CA: Corwin Press, www.corwinpress.com. Reproduction authorized only for the local school site or nonprofit organization that has purchased this book.

## Contextual

Practitioners reflecting at a contextual level should make up the majority of the group. They are able to analyze problems according to context, incorporating theory within practice and addressing the needs of students. The following two activities will assist practitioners in making observations of more complex situations, amending instruments to fit context, and interpreting data collected from observations.

## Task 11    Observing Effective Questioning

*Topic:* Observational learning

*Objective:* The practitioner will use an observational rating system to assess questioning effectiveness in a classroom situation.

*Materials:* Individual copies of Questioning Strategies (Table 3.2); clear transparencies (two for facilitator and one for each team); individual copies of Observational Checklist for Effective Questioning Strategies (Table 3.3); deck of playing cards

*Time:* Two 30-minute periods; one 15-minute classroom observation period

*Procedure:* Day 1

1. Distribute copies of Questioning Strategies. Discuss with practitioners questioning strategies that have been proven to be effective based on research findings.

2. Group practitioners into fours by randomly distributing playing cards (ace, king, queen, jack, etc.) to each participant.

3. Distribute a copy of Observational Checklist: Effective Questioning Strategies to each team. Allow 15 minutes for teams to discuss and amend the checklists to reflect classroom teaching assignments.

4. Instruct practitioners to use the Observational Checklist for a 15-minute observation period in each individual's field setting.

Day 2

1. Practitioners will be teamed in the same groups formed during the Day 1 activity. Each team will elect a leader. Allow 10 minutes for teams to collect thoughts on the value of the instrument created and used in recording desired data. Provide each team with a transparency on which to sketch the instrument.

2. Call on the leaders of each team in turn to briefly explain to the whole group their instrument and its value in determining questioning effectiveness in the classroom.

*Evaluation:* An observational rating system was used to assess questioning effectiveness in a classroom setting and the analysis of the instrument's use through group discussion.

*Debriefing:* 1. What are suggested ways of adapting the instrument to meet the practitioners' needs?

2. What needs prompted changes made in the instrument prior to use?

3. Why is it important to record only observable behaviors?

4. At what point are practitioners' inferences justifiable?

5. How might data collected from an observation instrument be used?

6. What are some possible advantages to using a checklist? Disadvantages?

**Table 3.2**    Questioning Strategies

- State questions briefly and clearly

- Ask one question at a time

- Provide at least 3 seconds of wait time

- Use a variety of questions

- Sequence questions

- Use higher-order questions

- Provide positive feedback

- Provide cues, if needed

- Encourage students to ask questions

- Require a response

Copyright © 2005 by Corwin Press. All rights reserved. Reprinted from *Promoting Reflective Thinking in Teachers: 50 Action Strategies,* by Germaine L. Taggart and Alfred P. Wilson. Thousand Oaks, CA: Corwin Press, www.corwinpress.com. Reproduction authorized only for the local school site or nonprofit organization that has purchased this book.

**Table 3.3**    Observation Checklist for Effective Questioning Strategies

| *Questioning Strategy* | *Check if Observed* |
|---|---|
| **State questions briefly and clearly** | _____ |
| **Ask one question at a time** | _____ |
| **Provide at least 3 seconds of wait time** | _____ |
| **Use a variety of questions** | _____ |
| **Sequence questions** | _____ |
| **Use higher-order questions** | _____ |
| **Provide positive feedback** | _____ |
| **Provide cues, if needed** | _____ |
| **Encourage students to ask questions** | _____ |
| **Require a response** | _____ |

Copyright © 2005 by Corwin Press. All rights reserved. Reprinted from *Promoting Reflective Thinking in Teachers: 50 Action Strategies,* by Germaine L. Taggart and Alfred P. Wilson. Thousand Oaks, CA: Corwin Press, www.corwinpress.com. Reproduction authorized only for the local school site or nonprofit organization that has purchased this book.

## Task 12    Observing Classroom Management Styles

*Topic:*    Observational learning

*Objective:*    The practitioner will use a narrative format while observing a current classroom environment to distinguish whether individual classroom management styles are low, moderate, or high teacher-control environments.

*Materials:*    Copy of Definition of Classroom Management (Table 3.4); Synopsis of Classroom Management Styles (Table 3.5); individual copies of Classroom Management Approaches (Table 3.6); Classroom Management Chart (Table 3.7), one copy per team of three; clear transparencies

*Time:*    One 45-minute period; one 15-minute classroom observation period; one 25-minute period

*Procedure:*    *Day 1*

1. Discuss with the whole group the definition of classroom management. Ask for factors that have helped to determine practitioners' management styles. List factors as presented on a clear transparency. Distribute and review briefly the Classroom Management Approaches handout to provide an overview of models to be discussed.

2. Group participants in teams of three by having them count off. Within each team, members will become experts on low, moderate, or high teacher-control environments. The tallest team member will become an expert at low-control environments, the shortest team member will become an expert at high-control environments, and the remaining team member will become an expert at moderate-control environments.

3. Practitioners will use a modified version of the Jigsaw approach (Aronson, Blaney, Stephan, Sikes, & Snapp, 1978), a strategy designed for processing divergent information. Practitioners from different teams who have corresponding environmental control topics form temporary groups called *expert groups.* Each expert group meets to discuss the characteristics of and approaches to the assigned environmental control topic. Distribute Synopsis of Classroom Management Styles for the expert groups to use as information and to prompt discussion of possible examples. Allow about 15 minutes.

4. Experts return to original teams to discuss the levels of environmental control within classroom management styles, with team members using the additional information and examples supplied by the expert groups. Allow 15 minutes.

5. Bring the whole group together to discuss management styles and examples considered by each team, and to answer any questions that may have developed.

6. Assign practitioners to observe a classroom situation for 15 minutes, recording in narrative format observations exemplifying low, moderate, or high teacher-control models. Observations will be discussed on Day 2.

*Day 2*

1. Allow original teams formed during Day 1 to have 10 minutes to analyze the findings of their observations.

2. As a whole group, discuss findings related to the control environments observed. Record observations and examples on the Classroom Management Chart.

*Evaluation:* Practitioners observed a classroom setting using a narrative format to document practices within the classroom indicative of low, moderate, or high teacher-control styles; they then discussed findings with the whole group.

*Debriefing:*

1. Was there a control level that seemed to be predominant? Explain possible reasons for this.

2. In which control level do you feel most comfortable? Why?

3. Was there evidence that the level of control changed with the context of a situation? What advantages and disadvantages might this change have?

4. Why is it important to record only observable behaviors?

5. At what point are practitioners' inferences justifiable?

6. How might data collected using a narrative format be used?

7. What are advantages and disadvantages to using a narrative format for documenting observations?

**Table 3.4**  Definition of Classroom Management

# Actions and strategies practitioners use to encourage students to act within acceptable limits so that achievement may be attained.

Copyright © 2005 by Corwin Press. All rights reserved. Reprinted from *Promoting Reflective Thinking in Teachers: 50 Action Strategies*, by Germaine L. Taggart and Alfred P. Wilson. Thousand Oaks, CA: Corwin Press, www.corwinpress.com. Reproduction authorized only for the local school site or nonprofit organization that has purchased this book.

**Table 3.5**    Synopsis of Classroom Management Styles

**Low Teacher Control**

The central philosophical beliefs behind the low teacher-control approach are that students are primarily responsible for controlling their behavior and that they have the capacity for decision making. The practitioner's responsibility is to structure the learning environment to facilitate students' control and learning and to enforce an orderly environment. Student autonomy is evidenced by their assistance in the development of expectations.

Proponents of low-control approaches are Berne, with his idea of transactional analysis, and Redl and Wattenberg's group management. Transactional analysis stems from questioning and analysis of verbal interactions. The approach was originated by Berne in his book, *Games People Play* (1964). Redl and Wattenberg's *Mental Hygiene in Teaching* (1959), later summarized by Redl in *When We Deal With Children* (1972), explains group management.

Berne contends that individuals possess three ego states—parent, child, and adult—which develop through life experiences and are either consciously or subconsciously held. The parent ego state pertains to parent and substitute parent influences that have helped us develop rules, norms, and mores. The child ego state develops from experiences in childhood, which tend to be more compulsive and expressive. The preferred adult ego state tends to provide rationality and problem-solving techniques for learners. Berne advocates that practitioners and students alike should strive to remain in this state to promote communication, positive relationships, and rational decision making.

Redl and Wattenberg advocate group management techniques to maintain control and to strengthen emotional development. The following are key features of the techniques.

Individuals act differently in groups than they do in individual settings.

Group dynamics vary within, between, and among groups.

Group behavior is determined by the perceptions of adult roles.

Diagnostic thinking can aid practitioners in determining underlying causes of behavior. Prior to practitioner interaction, determination of motivation, interaction dynamics, and potential future behaviors after intervention will foster positive responses.

**Moderate Teacher Control**

The central philosophical beliefs behind the moderate teacher-control approach are that practitioners and students are jointly responsible for controlling behavior and development, and that people are motivated by a need to belong and be accepted by others. The practitioner's responsibility is to structure the learning environment to facilitate students' control, yet place the needs of the group as a whole ahead of individual students' needs. The practitioners also enforce rules and assist students in recognizing consequences of decisions and actions. Students are provided with opportunities to control their behavior and to jointly develop classroom rules and consequences with the practitioner.

Proponents of moderate-control approaches are Dreikurs, who suggests logical consequences; Nelsen, who advocates *Positive Discipline* (1987); Glasser, who promotes reality therapy and control theory in *Schools Without Failure* (1969); and Kounin, who published *Discipline and Group Management in Classrooms* (1970). Dreikurs, using the work of Adler, supports the idea that acceptance is a large part of developmental success. Logical consequences—events arranged by the teacher that are directly and logically related to a behavior—are used extensively in Dreikurs's democratic approach. He identifies three techniques that lead to logical consequences: (1) Determine the goal for the behavior or misbehavior and confront the student with the goal for verification. (2) React to the misbehavior after rationally determining best alternatives for the action. Discussion of alternatives with the student is encouraged. (3) Use statements of encouragement to promote the use of positive alternatives. Nelsen adapts Dreikurs's approach into a program called *positive discipline.* In this program, kindness, respect, firmness, and encouragement are used to promoting positive behaviors. Key components include the following:

Natural and logical consequences that foster positive classroom atmosphere

Understanding that there are four goals in behavior: attention, power, revenge, and respect

Expression of kindness and firmness when dealing with misbehavior

Mutual respect

Use of family and class meetings

Encouragement that fosters self-evaluation

Glasser's ideology of classroom management has changed since his first book, *Schools Without Failure,* appeared in 1969. Initially, reality therapy promoted the idea that students were responsible for choices and that they must live with the natural consequences of those choices. Practitioners and students jointly prepare rules and consequences. Practitioners are responsible for enforcing the rules and consequences by requiring students to make value judgments

*(Continued)*

**Table 3.5** (Continued)

about misbehaviors. Practitioners are then responsible for suggesting possible consequences that are then discussed and agreed on by both the practitioner and the student. Control theory added the need to belong, to love, and to control, and the needs for freedom and fun to the existing philosophy of reality therapy. In 1992, Glasser published *The Quality School.* The central philosophy that supports meeting the needs of students was expanded to advocate that school management must be reorganized to help meet student needs and promote effective learning. *The Quality School Teacher* (1993) is Glasser's latest book and provides strategies for meeting the needs of students in quality schools.

The Kounin model, based upon a philosophy expressed in *Discipline and Group Management in Classrooms* (1970), describes lessons and management strategies that can be used to prevent and to address misbehavior. Kounin uses the term *withitness* to describe the reaction of teachers to misbehaviors in a timely and appropriate fashion. When referring to simultaneous misbehaviors, Kounin refers to *overlapping.* To be an effective practitioner, *withitness* during overlapping events is required.

Movement management is another key area in Kounin's philosophy. Momentum, pacing, and transition are essential skills controlled by the practitioner for maintaining classroom control. Kounin suggests that there are two mistakes related to movement management that cause practitioners difficulties. First, *jerkiness,* which refers to changes in the pacing of activities, prompts misbehavior. Second, *slowdowns* are delays or wasted moments that occur because of *overdwelling* or fragmentation. Other misbehaviors may occur because of satiation with a topic or because of a ripple effect of misbehaviors.

**High Teacher Control**

The central philosophical belief behind the high teacher-control approach is that students' growth and development are a result of external environmental conditions. The practitioner's responsibility is to select and reinforce desirable behaviors and extinguish undesirable behaviors. Few choices are given to students in this approach, as adults are seen as more capable of providing direction and making choices.

Proponents of high-control approaches are Skinner, Canter, and Dobson. Skinner is predominantly known for his philosophy of behavior modification first published in *Beyond Freedom and Dignity* (1971). Behavior modification involves reinforcement or punishment techniques for shaping behavior. The responsibility of the practitioners lies in providing reinforcements, or rewards, for desired behaviors and providing punishment for the performance of undesirable acts. Behavior modification is an organized, systematic model that must be applied consistently. Techniques of behavior modification include the following:

Catch them being good.

Ignore or praise rule breaking or keeping.

Reward or punish rule keeping or breaking.

Use contingency or "token" management systems.

Contract for desired behavior.

Canter and Canter's (1976) goal for assertive discipline is to teach students to act responsibly and by doing so, to increase self-esteem and academic success. The practitioner's roles are

To establish rules and directions that clearly define the limits of acceptable and unacceptable behavior

Teach the rules and directions

Request assistance from parents or administrators when needed

Canter's assertive discipline plan has three parts: establishment of rules, positive recognition that results from desirable behaviors, and consequences that result from misbehaviors.

Dobson (1970), in his book *Dare to Discipline*, maintains that healthy, happy children come from environments where there is a balance between love and control. Permissiveness is not allowed as children must be taught self-discipline and responsible behavior. Practitioners have the responsibility to establish boundaries and enforce consequences, giving children the "maximum reason to comply with your wishes" (p. 118). Dobson advocates infrequent use of corporal punishment in situations such as dangerous conditions, defiance, or temper tantrums. Preferred punishments are spanking, time-out, or loss of privileges.

SOURCE: Adapted from *Classroom Management and Discipline: Methods to Facilitate Cooperation and Instruction* by Paul R. Burden. Copyright © 1995 by Longman Publishers, USA. Reprinted by permission of Addison-Wesley Educational Publishers, Inc., by permission of Burden (1995).

**Table 3.6**    Classroom Management Approaches

| Level of Control | Level of Control | Proponents |
| --- | --- | --- |
| Low Teacher Control | Transactional analysis | Eric Berne |
| | Congruent communication | Fritz Redl |
| | Group management | William Wattenberg |
| Moderate Teacher Control | Logical consequences | Rudolph Dreikurs |
| | Encouragement | Jane Nelsen |
| | Cooperative discipline | William Glasser |
| | Reality therapy | Jacob Kounin |
| | Control therapy | |
| | Lesson and group management | |
| High Teacher Control | Structured classrooms | B. F. Skinner |
| | Behavior modification | Lee Canter |
| | Assertive discipline | James Dobson |
| | Corporal punishment | |

SOURCE: Adapted from *Classroom Management and Discipline: Methods to Facilitate Cooperation and Instruction* by Paul R. Burden. Copyright © 1995 by Longman Publishers USA. Reprinted by permission of Addison-Wesley Educational Publishers, Inc., by permission from Burden (1995).

**Table 3.7** Classroom Management Chart

| Type of Control | Indicators |
|---|---|
| Low | |
| Moderate | |
| High | |

Copyright © 2005 by Corwin Press. All rights reserved. Reprinted from *Promoting Reflective Thinking in Teachers: 50 Action Strategies*, by Germaine L. Taggart and Alfred P. Wilson. Thousand Oaks, CA: Corwin Press, www.corwinpress.com. Reproduction authorized only for the local school site or nonprofit organization that has purchased this book.

## Dialectical

Practitioners reflecting at a dialectical level address problems with self-confidence and incorporate moral, ethical, and sociopolitical issues into decision making. They welcome peer review and question actions in a constant quest for workable alternatives. The following two lessons will assist practitioners in making observations dealing with a wide scope of alternatives, collaborating to improve instruction, and interpreting data collected from observations.

## Task 13 Belief Systems: Their Role in Observational Learning

*Topic:* Observational learning

*Objective:* The practitioner will categorize observations made within a 15-minute period according to those activities necessary for instruction and those considered unnecessary based on current belief systems.

*Materials:* Observation Chart (Table 3.8); 3 × 5 index cards in three to five colors; one 5-ft. tall newsprint section attached to the wall for each team; markers

*Time:* One 30-minute period; one 15-minute peer classroom observation period; one 50-minute period

*Procedure:* *Day 1*

1.  Distribute a 3 × 5 colored note card to each practitioner. Practitioners will individually write five personal beliefs about educating students on their cards. Allow 5 minutes.

2.  Group practitioners into teams of three to five according to the color of note card on which beliefs were written.

3.  Allow team members to discuss commonalities and variances in beliefs. Encourage disclosure of past experiences that may have prompted the beliefs. Allow 20 minutes.

4.  Gather practitioners back into one large group. Distribute and briefly discuss the Observation Chart. The task for practitioners is to observe in a mentor's or team member's classroom for 15 minutes using the Observation Chart. The completed chart will be discussed on Day 2.

*Day 2*

1.  Practitioners are grouped in the same teams as on Day 1. Each team elects a leader. Allow 10 minutes for teams to discuss the observation instrument and results of the observation.

2.  Each team prepares a list of beliefs deemed important for successful achievement in the classroom. Record those beliefs using markers onto the newsprints hung about the room. Three or four observational indicators should be listed under each belief that supports the belief statement. Allow 15 minutes.

3.  Allow 15 minutes for teams to rotate clockwise about the room discussing listed beliefs and indicators. Look for commonalities and differences, with the leader recording comments.

4.  Call randomly on members of each team to briefly summarize the team's discussions.

*Evaluation:* Practitioners categorized observations according to belief systems and participated actively in team discussion.

*Debriefing:*   1.  What general statements can be made regarding the belief systems of practitioners in this session?

2.  Were indicators for some beliefs more difficult to observe than others?

3.  Which practitioners modified a belief statement based on observations? On team discussion?

4.  Which practitioners modified actions based on their observations and belief statements?

5.  Explain some of the universal beliefs regarding education.

**Table 3.8**   Observation Chart

| Observation | N | U | Belief System |
|---|---|---|---|
|  |  |  |  |
|  |  |  |  |
|  |  |  |  |
|  |  |  |  |
|  |  |  |  |
|  |  |  |  |
|  |  |  |  |
|  |  |  |  |
|  |  |  |  |
|  |  |  |  |
|  |  |  |  |
|  |  |  |  |
|  |  |  |  |

N = necessary; U = unnecessary

Copyright © 2005 by Corwin Press. All rights reserved. Reprinted from *Promoting Reflective Thinking in Teachers: 50 Action Strategies,* by Germaine L. Taggart and Alfred P. Wilson. Thousand Oaks, CA: Corwin Press, www.corwinpress.com. Reproduction authorized only for the local school site or nonprofit organization that has purchased this book.

## Task 14   Interpreting Change

| | |
|---|---|
| *Topic:* | Observational learning |
| *Objective:* | The practitioner will (a) reflect on a classroom event that illustrates a change in philosophy, practice, or attitude; (b) analyze and clarify reasons for the change; and (c) determine attitude toward the change. |
| *Materials:* | Notepaper and pen; Dimensions of Change document (either display copy or handouts, Table 3.9); clear transparencies |
| *Time:* | 40 minutes |
| *Procedure:* | |

1. Ask practitioners to freely write for a 5-minute period regarding an event observed or experienced in a classroom situation that illustrates a change in philosophy, practice, or attitude on their part.

2. Pair practitioners by allowing each person to work with a partner with whom they are comfortable so as to create a risk-free environment.

3. Discuss the Dimensions of Change document. Ask pairs of practitioners to view their writings in terms of these dimensions, taking notes on discussion elements. Allow 10 minutes.

4. Bring the whole group back together to discuss change. Endeavor to get practitioners to reflect on attitudes of change, possible reasons for change, and possible reasons not to change. Use a clear transparency on the overhead to list comments.

| | |
|---|---|
| *Evaluation:* | Practitioners reflected on change individually, in pairs, and in whole-group discussion. |
| *Debriefing:* | |

1. Why is change so difficult?

2. How were you able to make the change? Was it lasting? Why or why not?

3. What helps practitioners bring about lasting, meaningful change?

4. Express your views on the dimensions of change.

5. Explain the value of spending time and effort toward changing to reflective thinking.

**Table 3.9**     Dimensions of Change

*Change*

- Is multidimensional

- Varies within individuals as well as within groups

- Involves skills, practice, attitudes, and theory

- Relates to occupational identity, sense of competency, and self-concept

- Consists of dynamic interrelationships between and among other dimensions

- Must be defined relative to concrete individuals and situations

- Must have sound reasons behind it

- Is difficult to achieve with any depth

- Must be of value to be meaningful

Excerpted with permission of publisher from Fullan, M. G., with Stigelbauer, S., *The New Meaning of Educational Change, 2nd Ed.* (New York: Teachers College Press, © 1991 by Teachers College, Columbia University. All rights reserved.) p. 198.

# REFLECTIVE QUESTIONS

1. How can observational learning be better used in existing classroom situations?

2. Explain the place of observational learning in the field of administration.

3. What aspects of observational learning are the most beneficial to your continued growth in reflective thinking?

# ACTION ASSIGNMENTS

## Technical

1. Experience additional controlled observation sessions using taped vignettes.

2. Observe a child's exploration of new uses for old objects in a classroom situation (e.g., old socks for puppets, Styrofoam cups for gardens, etc.).

## Contextual

1. Observe appropriate uses of cooperative learning strategies, using a narrative form of documentation. Discuss instrumentation that would make this observational learning process easier (e.g., a tally chart listing the key components of cooperative learning as the observational focus).

2. Observe student and practitioner experiences and reactions to the use of new manipulative devices (e.g., use of Cuisenaire rods in making fraction trains for determining equivalent fractions).

## Dialectical

1. Experience additional controlled observations using taped vignettes that deal with ethical issues in teaching.

2. Consider the moral, ethical, and sociopolitical implications of classroom observation.

# SUGGESTIONS FOR SUCCESS

1. Provide a risk-free environment.

2. Allow ample time for discussion of observations.

3. Simplify the instrument. Some practitioners find that the observation instrument for assessing clear directions is too complex. It may be necessary to break the instrument into more manageable components, especially for preservice practitioners.

## JOURNALING REFLECTIVE GROWTH

1. How can classroom observations increase reflective thinking?

2. Explain the aspects of observational learning that you would feel comfortable using in the classroom on an ongoing basis. What could be done to facilitate the aspects of observational learning that you feel uncomfortable using in the classroom?

3. Explain your growth in your ability to reflect.

# 4

# Writing Reflective Journals

*I am struck continually by the isolation, the loneliness of teaching. The dialogue journal is one way to alter this isolation, and as such, it represents an essential human truth: we become and remain human not through the acquisition of factual knowledge or skills, but through participation in social communities.*

—Staton (1987, p. 60)

---

### Chapter Objectives

**The facilitator will**

- Assist practitioners in demonstrating proficiency in the use of the journaling strategy
- Be able to assess growth in reflective thinking on application of the strategy
- Analyze personal competence with the strategy to assist practitioners in preparing action plans that will foster personal reflection on return to the classroom situation
- Facilitate maintenance of reflective journals to be used by practitioners for personal growth assessment and for peer assessment

---

## THE USE OF REFLECTIVE JOURNALS

Posner (1996) states that more learning is derived from reflecting on an experience than from the experience itself. Reflective journaling assists practitioners by making practice more educative, reveals Oberg (as cited in Clift, Houston, &

Pugach, 1990). Educative practice provides consistency between practice and the beliefs and values of practitioners.

The type of journal used by this author for the purpose of enhancing reflective thinking is the dialogue journal. Copeland (as cited in Clift et al., 1990) cautions that journal writing contributes to reflection when practitioners are taught journaling techniques and receive thoughtful, meaningful feedback. The dialogue journal allows the reflective practitioner to gain the benefits of journal writing. In addition, it provides facilitators with a tool for responding to events and to reflections on events by practitioners. Dialogue occurs when the facilitator responds to journal entries either through discussion or through written entries. Written entries may be made in the margins of the journal or on Post-it notes for placement in the journal. Care should be taken by the practitioner and facilitator to maintain subject anonymity and educational integrity. Responding to journaling may seem overwhelming. However, responding to a few journals a day or collecting journals periodically for responses will make the task manageable.

The dialogue journal is a widely used method of recording events and personal vignettes. The journal provides its author with an opportunity to chronicle over a period of time, then reflect on events. Dialogue journals may describe the episode, analyze cause and effect, and attempt to determine roles and beliefs stemming from the event. Assumptions and responses may be noted and analyzed as well as relationships between the event and traditionally held beliefs, traditions, or theories. For clarity of documentation, it is best that the dialogue journal entry be made as soon as possible following the event. Subsequent notes may be made at later dates once the initial entry has been written (Posner, 1996).

Norton (1994) contends that explicit guidelines; topics that compliment discussions and vice versa; and extensive, probing feedback from the mentor responding to the journal are instrumental in development of reflective thinking through journal writing. According to Posner (1996), a general format for dialogue journals would include

- Date and time of the entry
- Brief sequencing of the events of the day
- Elaboration on details of one or two episodes based on level of excitement, puzzlement, or confirmation
- Analysis of the episode
  - Possible explanations for the event
  - Significance of the event
  - What was learned
  - Questions raised
  - Relevance
  - Responsibility on the part of the practitioner

Journal use has many benefits in promoting reflective thinking (Bolin, 1988; Copeland, as cited in Clift et al., 1990; Garman, 1986; Houston & Clift,

1990; Yinger & Clark, 1981; Zeichner & Liston, 1987; Zinsser, 1988). Journals provide the reflective practitioner with a means of

- Analyzing and reasoning through a dilemma
- Enhancing development and reflection
- Promoting growth in critical analysis of teaching
- Promoting awareness of relationships between educational psychology and practical experiences
- Systematically reflecting on self-development and on actions within classroom and work contexts
- Practicing reflective inquiry
- Building understanding by writing about what is learned
- Linking understanding with classroom practice

Journals provide the facilitator with a means of

- Challenging, supporting, and monitoring a practitioner's reflective thinking
- Promoting questions and discussion in educational course work and field experiences
- Analyzing teacher development, learning perspectives, and current level of understanding
- Guiding instruction
- Qualitatively analyzing instruction or a program
- Effectively maximizing staff development

The facilitator promotes discussion of the use and value of dialogue journals as a learning and reflective tool. Activities are written at each of the three reflective levels: technical, contextual, and dialectical. Activities selected should be based on the experiences of the practitioners and the levels of reflective thinking as determined by the Profile of Reflective Thinking Attributes (see Form 2.1). Level of reflection within journal entries may be determined by using the authors' Reflective Thinking Pyramid (see Figure 1.1), Sparks-Langer et al.'s (1991) Framework for Reflective Thinking (see Table 2.1), or Hattan and Smith's (1995) writing analysis guidelines described in Chapter 2.

## REFLECTIVE ACTIVITIES

### Technical

At a technical level, practitioners have not had many experiences from which to formulate solutions to problematic classroom situations. The following activities will assist practitioners in organizing observations into a format that promotes reflective thinking, by raising levels of awareness and meaning of observations and by providing documentation from which information can be gathered for group discussion.

## Task 15    Formatting a Journal Entry

*Topic:* Reflective journaling

*Objective:* The practitioner will analyze journal entries to develop a general format for preparing them.

*Materials:* Transparency of Journal Entry (Table 4.1); individual copies of Journal Entry I and Journal Entry II (Tables 4.2 and 4.3); transparency of Benefits of Using Reflective Journals (Table 4.4); transparency and individual copies of Dialogue Journal Format (Table 4.5); clear transparencies

*Time:* 60 minutes

*Procedure:* 1. In a whole group, discuss with practitioners the benefits of journaling (Table 4.4). Inform practitioners that when first starting to use a journal, it is often best to follow a specific format until a comfort level is reached.

2. Read Journal Entry (Table 4.1) to practitioners as they view it on the overhead projector. On a clear transparency, list practitioner suggestions from the journal entry that would make journaling easier. Possible suggestions are listed on the Dialogue Journal Format (Table 4.5).

3. When brainstorming on format items is complete (allow 5 minutes), place the Dialogue Journal Format on the overhead projector. Distribute copies and discuss format with practitioners.

4. Distribute copies of Journal Entry I and Journal Entry II. Ask practitioners to choose a partner with whom to review journal entries to determine if format was followed. The person with the longest hair in each group will then report discussion results.

5. Use the Dialogue Journal Format (Table 4.5) on the overhead projector to discuss with the whole group the benefits of such a format and the value of the format to novice journal writers.

*Evaluation:* Practitioners became acquainted with journal format by analyzing journal entries.

*Debriefing:* 1. How might the journaling format be amended to fit time constraints?

2. By using a set format, do you feel reflection is helped or hindered? Explain your response.

3. Do you agree with the statement, "When people write about something, they learn it better"? Explain your response.

4. What type of response from your supervisor or peer would you most like to see written in your dialogue journal?

**Table 4.1**    Journal Entry

November 12                    8:30 A.M.

Today the students had an Awards Assembly. Certain individuals were given awards for being good citizens, missing no school, and so forth. I think this is another neat thing this school does. It gives the students a sense of pride and helps build self-esteem. This reinforcement encourages positive behaviors that will stay with these individuals for a lifetime. Building self-esteem is so important at this age level as well as other developmental stages.

With the short amount of class time left, the teacher taught the students to count by fives. Since we were studying about Pilgrims, and there were 102 Pilgrims on the *Mayflower* when it came to America, we counted by fives up to 100, then added two to make 102.

Chris

Copyright © 2005 by Corwin Press. All rights reserved. Reprinted from *Promoting Reflective Thinking in Teachers: 50 Action Strategies,* by Germaine L. Taggart and Alfred P. Wilson. Thousand Oaks, CA: Corwin Press, www.corwinpress.com. Reproduction authorized only for the local school site or nonprofit organization that has purchased this book.

**Table 4.2**   Journal Entry I

November 9      8:30–10:00 A.M.

Today, Ms. W. had a substitute teacher. It was a great experience for me because I saw from direct observation what a substitute teacher deals with as well as what Ms. W. comes back to. I guess this is when a teacher's flexibility comes in. We started the morning with Total Reading. The substitute knew a little background on it because her daughter goes to first grade in the same building. However, she did not approach it like Ms. W., which bothered the children. The children let her know she wasn't saying the chants fast enough. She also did not write phrases on the board correctly. (Ms. W. usually has a lined ruling and demonstrates exactly how it should look on the paper.) Finally, she hardly knew any hand signals, which some of the children depend on. I know it would be impossible for her to do things like Ms. W., but it really seemed to bother the children and affected their performance.

We also didn't get everything done that we were supposed to. I'm sure Ms. W. gave us plenty, though, so we wouldn't run out of things to do. A few directions were also vague, which made it difficult to know what she wanted. We basically followed the same routine, and the children were pretty good. They definitely let the substitute know when she wasn't doing something right. I think it would be very difficult to be a substitute teacher, because there is no way to prepare, and he or she walks into the classroom blind. Also, Ms. W. will have to readjust to whatever didn't get done or wasn't done right. Even though it was a little frustrating and chaotic, I'm glad I had this experience. It was a real eye-opener!

Dean

Copyright © 2005 by Corwin Press. All rights reserved. Reprinted from *Promoting Reflective Thinking in Teachers: 50 Action Strategies*, by Germaine L. Taggart and Alfred P. Wilson. Thousand Oaks, CA: Corwin Press, www.corwinpress.com. Reproduction authorized only for the local school site or nonprofit organization that has purchased this book.

**Table 4.3**   Journal Entry II

November 13       7:30–10:00 A.M.

Faculty Meeting

Journaling

Work on reports

I began the day by attending a faculty meeting. Every Monday morning, the faculty has a meeting from 7:30 A.M. till about 9:00 A.M. A parent stays and supervises each home room during this time. I think this is a good idea, for the faculty to meet and discuss issues every week. On Monday, there is a different schedule due to this meeting.

When the students arrived for class, I was surprised by the various sizes of the students. There was quite a range for the same age and grade level. I was also surprised by how the students behaved. They were relatively quiet as they went about their business. When following directions, the students again were quiet and got right to the point. If any talking was going on, it was through a light whisper.

Next, the class wrote on a given topic in their journals. The teacher does not read what they write but makes sure that each entry is at least seven lines. They have 5 minutes to complete their entry and are timed with a timer. This process is done at the beginning of every class period. While observing, I noticed a couple of boys not writing very much. I was surprised by this. These are easy points to receive. All the teacher wants from them is to count the number of lines. All it takes for the students to receive the points is a small effort. Yet some of the students don't care enough to make that effort. A boy from another class didn't even write anything. He just drew a picture. Even after he realized that the teacher and I knew what he was doing, he continued drawing. When it was time to put the journals away, he proudly showed one of his friends the drawing. It was clear to me that he did this for attention and to impress his fellow students. I was amazed!

Every Monday morning, the teacher writes the weekly agenda on the board. The students are given time to copy it into their agenda notebooks. The school supplies each student with one of these notebooks. I think this is a super idea! What a great way to prepare students for high school and college. It is also a great way to promote responsibility and teach organizational skills. I was really impressed by this idea!

The students had short stories that were due. They had the opportunity to either (a) read their short story aloud themselves, (b) have the teacher read their stories without telling who wrote them, or (c) not have them read at all. The teacher had planned on the students responding, but only one student had his paper read. I was really impressed with his paper. It was 17 pages long (typed) and had a high vocabulary content. The teacher had to change her plans since no one wanted their stories read. She sent them to the library instead, which she originally had planned for tomorrow. Once again, teachers need to be flexible! I have to say I wasn't really surprised by the response the teacher received. The students are at an age where they would be embarrassed or self-conscious. They are too worried about what their peers might think.

One other thing I would like to comment on is that I think middle school lessons are easier to prepare. The teacher did the exact same thing every class period. She only had to prepare for one lesson, whereas an elementary teacher has to prepare for several. It is clear it takes more preparation for an elementary teacher than a middle school one.

Ann

Copyright © 2005 by Corwin Press. All rights reserved. Reprinted from *Promoting Reflective Thinking in Teachers: 50 Action Strategies*, by Germaine L. Taggart and Alfred P. Wilson. Thousand Oaks, CA: Corwin Press, www.corwinpress.com. Reproduction authorized only for the local school site or nonprofit organization that has purchased this book.

**Table 4.4**     Benefits of Using Reflective Journals

- Analyzing and reasoning through a dilemma

- Enhancing development and reflection

- Promoting growth in critical analysis of teaching

- Promoting awareness of relationships between educational psychology and practical experiences

- Systematically reflecting on self-development and on actions within classroom and work contexts

- Practicing reflective inquiry

- Building understanding by writing about what is learned

- Linking understanding with classroom practice

Copyright © 2005 by Corwin Press. All rights reserved. Reprinted from *Promoting Reflective Thinking in Teachers: 50 Action Strategies,* by Germaine L. Taggart and Alfred P. Wilson. Thousand Oaks, CA: Corwin Press, www.corwinpress.com. Reproduction authorized only for the local school site or nonprofit organization that has purchased this book.

**Table 4.5**     Dialogue Journal Format

- Date and time of the entry

- Brief sequencing of the events of the day

- Elaboration on details of one or two episodes based on level of excitement, puzzlement, or confirmation

- Analysis of the episode: possible explanations for event, significance of the event, what was learned, questions raised, relevance

SOURCE: Adapted from Posner (1996), *Field Experience: A Guide to Reflective Thinking.* © Addison-Wesley; reprinted by permission of Addison-Wesley.

## Task 16    Journaling the Reflective Thinking Process

*Topic:* Reflective journaling

*Objective:* The practitioner will observe a classroom environment to document instances of the use of the Reflective Thinking Model.

*Materials:* Display copy of Reflective Thinking Model (Figure 1.2); individual copies of Dialogue Journal Format (Table 4.5); individual copies of Journal Entry II (Table 4.3)

*Time:* Two 30-minute periods; one 15-minute classroom observation period

*Procedure:* *Day 1*

Note: Norton (1994) lists two requirements when using dialogue journaling as a catalyst for promoting and refining reflective thinking: (a) explicit format and (b) journal topics that are discussed or responded to on an ongoing basis. This is especially critical when dealing with particular problems.

1. Distribute the Dialogue Journal Format.

2. Review the Reflective Thinking Model with practitioners.

3. Group practitioners in pairs by asking them to partner with a colleague. The leader of each group will be the practitioner with the longest time in his or her current field setting.

4. Distribute copies of Journal Entry II. Instruct practitioners to read the journal entry to ascertain the use of the Reflective Thinking Model by the individual observed. Allow 10 minutes.

5. Discuss in a whole group the findings of each pair by calling on the leaders to report on each team's discussion.

6. Assign practitioners a 15-minute classroom observation period with the intent of journaling instances using the Reflective Thinking Model. Journal entries will be discussed on Day 2.

*Day 2*

1. Allow 10 minutes for the pairs formed on Day 1 to meet regarding their findings and journal entries.

2. Select two or three teams to role-play the reflective thinking process observed and journaled by one of the team members.

3. Use the Reflective Thinking Model to evaluate the process used.

*Evaluation:* Practitioners observed, journaled, and dialogued about the use of the reflective thinking model in the classroom.

*Debriefing:*   1.  How difficult was it to observe the use of the Reflective Thinking Model?

2.  Explain the usefulness of the Reflective Thinking Model in journaling episodes.

3.  Explain the usefulness of role-playing and discussion in clarifying the Reflective Thinking Model.

4.  How might observation and journaling make you a more effective practitioner? A more reflective practitioner?

## Contextual

Practitioners reflecting at a contextual level are able to observe a classroom situation, analyze episodes based on context, assess appropriateness of actions relative to the needs of students, and relate actions to a theoretical base. The following two activities will assist practitioners in using journaling and feedback to analyze complex situations, comparing and contrasting episodes dealing with a like concept, and interpreting the relationship between practice and theory.

| **Task 17** | **A Comparison of the Use of Journaling to an Observational Checklist** |

Topic: Reflective journaling

Objective: The practitioner will observe a classroom situation to record an episode involving clarity in giving directions, using an observation instrument or journaling. Comparison of the actions recorded will be made through group discussions.

Materials: Individual copies (enough for half of the practitioners) of Observational Checklist of Behaviors Indicative of Giving Clear Directions (Table 4.6); individual copies (enough for half of the practitioners) of Dialogue Journal Format (Table 4.5); two journal entries volunteered by practitioners copied onto clear transparencies; clear transparencies

Time: Two 30-minute periods; one 15-minute classroom observation period

Procedure: Day 1

1. Distribute Dialogue Journal Format to half of the practitioners and the Observational Checklist of Behaviors Indicative of Giving Clear Directions to the other half. Instruct practitioners possessing the Dialogue Journal Format to pair up with someone holding the Observational Checklist. Explain that they will be making observations regarding giving directions using one of the two techniques for recording.

2. Allow pairs of practitioners 5 minutes to compare advantages and disadvantages of the two techniques and to decide who will be the recorder and who will be the reporter for their team.

3. Discuss in the whole group the comparisons derived from the small-group discussions. List, using clear transparencies, advantages and disadvantages of each technique.

4. Instruct practitioners to use the observation instrument or journal for a 15-minute period in individual classroom assignments, observing the quality of directions presented to students.

Day 2

1. Allow 5 minutes for the pairs formed on Day 1 to meet regarding their findings on the use and value of each of the techniques.

2. Call on the reporter in several of the pairs to summarize the findings of the team. Allow other pairs to report, if desired.

Evaluation: Reflective comparisons were made of using an observational checklist versus a journal format to record a classroom episode involving clarity in giving directions.

Debriefing: 1. Which individuals are more likely to prefer the checklist technique over journaling? What are possible reasons for this?

2. As a reflective practitioner, state your preferred technique. Defend your choice.

3. The theory behind effective questioning is supported by research. How does the theory relate to actual classroom practice?

4. How do you know when your reflective thinking ability is improving?

**Table 4.6**     Observational Checklist of Behaviors Indicative of Giving Clear
Directions

*Directions*: Place a tally mark in the right-hand column each time an observation of the indicator is made during the observation period.

| *Behavior Indicator Observed* | *Tally* |
|---|---|
| Steps are provided in a logical sequence | _____ |
|    1.  Presented visually | _____ |
|    2.  Presented verbally | _____ |
| Steps are explained in detail | _____ |
|    1.  Full explanation given | _____ |
|    2.  Further explanation given, if necessary | _____ |
|    3.  Steps repeated, if necessary | _____ |
| Vocabulary is appropriate for developmental level | _____ |
| Steps are presented in a clear tone | _____ |
| Steps are presented at an appropriate volume | _____ |
| Steps are modeled for the students | _____ |
|    1.  Each step in process shown visually | _____ |
|    2.  Each step in process restated | _____ |
| Students are encouraged to ask questions | _____ |
|    1.  Through a verbal request | _____ |
|    2.  Through teacher body language | _____ |
| Students are asked questions to check for understanding | _____ |
|    1.  Students called upon randomly | _____ |
|    2.  Students called upon equitably | _____ |
|    3.  Students asked clarifying questions, if needed | _____ |

Copyright © 2005 by Corwin Press. All rights reserved. Reprinted from *Promoting Reflective Thinking in Teachers: 50 Action Strategies,* by Germaine L. Taggart and Alfred P. Wilson. Thousand Oaks, CA: Corwin Press, www.corwinpress.com. Reproduction authorized only for the local school site or nonprofit organization that has purchased this book.

## Task 18    A Comparison of Observations Recorded With and Without the Use of a Journaling Format

*Topic:* Reflective journaling

*Objective:* The practitioner will observe a classroom situation to record an episode involving clarity in giving directions. Half the practitioners will use a set journaling format and half will use a format of their choice. Comparison of the actions recorded will be made through group discussions.

*Materials:* Individual copies (enough for half the practitioners) of Dialogue Journal Format (Table 4.5); two journal entries volunteered by practitioners, one from each team, copied onto clear transparencies; clear transparencies

*Time:* Two 30-minute periods; one 15-minute classroom observation period

*Procedure:* *Day 1*

1. Distribute Dialogue Journal Format to half of the practitioners. Practitioners are not to share the format with others at this time. Explain that practitioners will be making observations regarding giving directions. Half will be using the journaling format; the other half will be free to use a format of their choice while making classroom observations.

2. Direct practitioners possessing the format to pair up and those possessing no format to do the same. Allow 15 minutes for teams to discuss how they would go about recording observations made.

3. Assign practitioners to record observations for a 15-minute period in individual classroom assignments, observing the quality of directions presented to children.

*Day 2*

1. Allow 15 minutes for the teams assigned on Day 1 to meet regarding their findings on the journaling activity. Discuss advantages and disadvantages to using a journaling format while recording observations. Teams should also select a leader, such as the individual who has the longest journal entry.

2. Call on the leader to summarize the findings of the team. Clear transparencies may be used to categorize advantages and disadvantages.

*Evaluation:* Reflective comparisons of observations of an episode involving clarity in giving directions were made, with and without using a journaling format.

*Debriefing:* 1. Which individuals are more likely to prefer using a prescribed format? What are possible reasons for this?

2. As a reflective practitioner, state your preferred technique. Defend your choice.

3. The theory behind effective questioning is supported by research. How does the theory relate to actual classroom practice?

4. How do you know when your reflective thinking ability is improving?

### Dialectical

Practitioners reflecting at a dialectical level address problems with self-confidence and incorporate moral, ethical, and sociopolitical issues into decision making. Peer review is welcomed as actions are constantly reviewed and updated as alternatives are sought. For these reasons, the following two lessons are open-ended. Practitioners will be assisted in making choices reflecting a wide variety of issues and alternatives.

## *Task 19*    **Open-Ended Journaling**

*Topic:* Reflective journaling

*Objective:* The practitioner will devise a system of journaling that meets instructional needs and addresses issues on a dialectical level.

*Materials:* Prepared individual copies of Benefits of Using Reflective Journals (Table 4.4); clear transparencies

*Time:* Two 30-minute periods; three 15-minute classroom observation periods

*Procedure:* *Day 1*

1. Prepare Benefits of Using Reflective Journals sheets by writing one of these terms at the bottom of each sheet: *change, instructional innovation, professionalism, collegiality,* or *decision making.*

2. Discuss with whole group the benefits of journaling and distribute Benefits of Using Reflective Journals sheets.

3. Group practitioners into teams of three or four according to the terms written at the bottom of their handouts. Teams are to devise a journaling format to use in observing and addressing an issue under the general term for each team. For example, the team with the term *change* may devise a plan to observe and journal episodes involving such models as constructivism or team teaching. Allow 20 minutes.

4. In whole-group discussion, summarize the efforts of the teams. Discuss problem areas, challenges, and expectations.

5. Assign practitioners to observe in a mentor or team member's classroom or school for three 15-minute periods and record observations that center around the issue using the journaling format devised.

*Day 2*

1. Practitioners will be grouped in the same teams formed on Day 1. Each team will select a leader. Allow 15 minutes for teams to discuss topics, findings, and journaling processes.

2. Each team will use a clear transparency to illustrate its journaling format and the findings of its observations. The team leader will report findings to the whole group using the transparencies.

*Evaluation:* Practitioners prepared and used a journaling format to appropriately address the topic assigned.

*Debriefing:* 1. What differences were noted in the various journaling formats presented? Similarities?

2. Is it necessary to be flexible in using a journaling format? Explain your rationale.

3. What made the topics presented challenging (or unchallenging) to observe and journal?

4. What other topic(s) would be of interest to you?

5. How can journaling efforts lead into action research?

### *Task 20*  **Rights and Responsibilities**

*Topic:* Reflective journaling

*Objective:* The practitioner will journal about events at an educational gathering, reflecting on the rights and responsibilities of practitioners.

*Materials:* Five 3-newsprint sheets hung about the room, each labeled with one of the following terms: *community, parent empowerment, ethical issues, legal issues,* and *lifelong learning;* markers; clear transparencies

*Time:* One 45-minute period, one 15-minute observation period, and one 30-minute period

*Procedure:* Day 1

1. Group practitioners by having them move to one of the five newsprint sheets that most reflects a personal concern. Provide each group with a marker. Designate the practitioner with the lightest hair color as the reporter, the one with the darkest hair color as the recorder.

2. Groups are to discuss the term designated on the newsprint to determine one or two specific issues within that topic they would like to address.

3. Each group is to format a plan for each team member to observe and journal one episode related to one or both specific issues. The episode must be taken from an event outside of regular classroom situations, for example, study groups, school board meetings, parent-teacher association meetings, university courses, and so on.

4. The recorder will write the chosen format on the newsprint.

5. Bring the practitioners together into a whole group. Each reporter will advise the group of his or her team plan.

6. Discuss challenges and concerns.

7. Assign each practitioner to observe in an educational setting for one 15-minute period and record observations that center around the issue chosen by the team using the format devised.

Day 2

1. Group practitioners in the same teams formed in Day 1. Allow 15 minutes for teams to discuss topics, findings, and journaling processes.

2. Each team will use a clear transparency to illustrate the journaling format and the findings of its observations. The team leader will report findings to the whole group using clear transparencies.

*Evaluation:* Practitioners prepared and used a journaling format to make observations on a chosen topic.

*Debriefing:*   1.  What differences were noted in the various journaling formats presented? Similarities?

2.  Is it necessary to be flexible in using a journaling format? Explain your rationale.

3.  Were the topics presented challenging to observe and journal? If so, what made them so?

4.  What other topic(s) would be of interest to you?

5.  How can journaling efforts lead to action research?

# REFLECTIVE QUESTIONS

1. How will journaling on a daily basis affect your teaching ability?

2. Identify a specific journal format that fits your personal needs better than others.

3. How do you feel about someone else reading and responding to your journal?

4. What actions may be taken as a result of journaled information?

5. What ethical and legal reasons support maintaining the anonymity of locations and individuals discussed in journal entries?

# ACTION ASSIGNMENTS

## Technical

1. Experience additional controlled observations and journaling practice using taped vignettes.

2. Collect journal entries from willing practitioners, remove the names, and make copies for review by other practitioners. Analyze the entries for format and level of reflection.

## Contextual

1. Observe one or two children with behavior problems in the classroom. Use journal entries over a period of time coupled with possible interventions to help determine the value of the interventions in controlling the unwanted behaviors.

2. Obtain permission to walk into a classroom in which you have never been. During the first 5 minutes after your arrival, journal all you can regarding the physical environment of the room. Later, analyze your entry: Why were the items mentioned noticed in that short time period? How is this relevant to your own classroom situation?

## Dialectical

1. Conduct additional observations of individuals: principals, superintendents, school psychologists and so on. Determine the role of these individuals in the school community. Do the roles determined differ from preconceived notions? Why is that so?

2. Journal about a negotiations meeting held by a local school district. Write only observable information. When the meeting is completed, add inferences gleaned from the observations. Is your perspective on the events of the meeting the same on reflection as during the time of your journaling?

## SUGGESTIONS FOR SUCCESS

1. Start small. Use a format and controlled situations. Graduate to less formality and more complex situations.

2. Practitioners should periodically review journal entries to assess growth in knowledge, skills, and reflective thinking ability.

## JOURNALING REFLECTIVE GROWTH

1. Will my use of journaling differ in the future because of increased knowledge about journaling?

2. Journaling is considered to be a form of reflection-on-action (Schön, 1987). An ultimate goal for reflective thinking is reflection-*in*-action. Do you feel that journaling will lead to reflection-in-action on your part? Why do you feel as you do?

3. Through journaling efforts thus far, are there topics that have sparked an interest for continued research? What are those topics? Will they lend themselves to action research?

# 5

# Using Practicum Strategies

*Reflection becomes the essential link between lessons and proves to be the difference between teaching to meet district objectives and teaching to help all students understand.*

—Schroeder (1996, p. 648)

---

### Chapter Objectives

**The facilitator will**

- Assist practitioners in demonstrating proficiency in the use of the practicum strategy
- Be able to assess growth in reflective thinking upon application of the strategy
- Analyze personal competence of the strategy to assist practitioners in preparing an action plan that will foster personal reflection upon return to the classroom situation
- Facilitate maintenance of reflective journals to be used by practitioners for personal growth assessment and for peer assessment

---

Two practicum strategies will be discussed in this section: *microteaching* and *reflective teaching*, popularized by Cruickshank (1985). Both strategies provide practitioners with opportunities to plan and implement lessons, present the lessons to small cohort groups, then reflect on the outcome of the presentations. Lessons are usually brief, 5 to 15 minutes long, and cover a single teaching concept. The experience is low risk. The benefits, however, are high when the practicum experience is followed by thoughtful facilitator-, peer-, and self-reflection.

## THE MICROTEACHING PROCESS

Microteaching has been a part of teacher preparation for the past three decades. As the name implies, microteaching is a simulated teaching experience of short duration, with the practitioner teaching a lesson to a small cohort group or to a small class of students. Orlich, Harder, Callahan, Kauchak, and Gibson (1994) provide the following rationale for the microteaching experience. Microteaching allows the practitioner to

- Practice a technique, strategy, or procedure
- Reduce anxiety by practicing in a supportive environment
- Test innovative approaches to a teaching concept
- Develop specific delivery strategies, such as questioning or closure
- Experience facilitator-, peer-, and self-evaluation
- Gain immediate feedback from experiences
- Practice team teaching in a supportive environment

The procedure for teaching a microteaching lesson is simple. The practitioner first decides on the topic or process to teach and prepares a plan for the lesson. The format of the lesson is preestablished. Specific performance objectives are outlined on the plan as well as materials needed, time constraints, and procedures for teaching the lesson. A conclusion and evaluation of the lesson's effectiveness in producing the desired objective ends the lesson. The practitioner rehearses the lesson; prepares two copies of the plan, one to refer to while teaching, and the other for the facilitator or peer; then teaches the lesson during a preset time period.

During the teaching experience, three formative evaluations are taking place. The first is the assessment of the microteaching by the facilitator. Using the copy of the plan, the facilitator should make written comments on the effectiveness of the plan in covering the objective, its portability, and the implementation of the plan by the practitioner. Be positive regarding strategies and concepts effectively used. Note improvements needed in a constructive manner.

The second formative evaluation is conducted simultaneously. One or more peers of the practitioner are also rating the microteaching. They, however, do not have access to the lesson plan. Both the facilitator and peer reviewers should rate the practitioner using the rubric prepared by the group prior to the microteaching experience (see Task 23).

Rubrics are used as an assessment tool. The rubric created by the practitioners provides a format for review of the teaching process. It allows for the practitioner to think about the important elements of the teaching episode and to reflect on teaching efficiencies and deficits. Ownership in the rubric is inherent in the fact that all practitioners participate in its construction (Taggart, Phifer, Nixon, & Wood, 1998).

During the course of the microteaching, the lesson is videotaped by a peer or technician. The goal of videotaping is to capture the interactions in the classroom. Once the novelty wears off, both students and teacher accept the presence of the equipment and the technician, and the class proceeds with minimal disruptions. Later, the videotaped lesson is reviewed by the practitioners, who use the rubric for microteaching to critique their own lesson. The critiquing session may be handled privately by the practitioner as the third formative assessment. This review should be accomplished soon after the microteaching event. The tape and critique are reviewed at a later date simultaneously by the facilitator and practitioner. The practitioner explains his or her critique using the rubric, the video is viewed with comments made by either the practitioner or the facilitator, and the lesson plan with facilitator comments and peer critiques is given to the practitioner. It is at this time that a final grade determination is made, if needed, and that goals are established for the next microteaching task.

## REFLECTIVE TEACHING

An alternative peer teaching experience to microteaching is reflective teaching, developed by Cruickshank, Kennedy, Williams, Holton, and Fay (1981) at Ohio State University. Reflective teaching is a strategy for promoting thinking about the process of teaching. It was developed as a peer teaching technique with the intent of making teachers more thoughtful practitioners (Cruickshank et al., 1981).

Cruickshank et al.'s reflective teaching is intended to promote method and efficiency. The method has won the support of professional organizations, such as Phi Delta Kappa and the American Association of Colleges for Teacher Education, because of its use as a viable experiential teaching alternative. The major aims of the reflective teaching approach (Cruickshank, 1985; Cruickshank et al., 1981; see Table 5.1) are

- To provide a controlled clinical atmosphere with which to practice instructional skills
- To provide an opportunity to consider a teaching episode thoughtfully, analytically, and objectively
- To develop habits of reflective thought about teaching
- To provide for peer teaching
- To provide the designated teacher with immediate feedback and reflection opportunities
- To provide an easily transportable alternative teaching model requiring few materials and limited time and space

**Table 5.1**     Aims of Reflective Teaching

- To provide a controlled clinical atmosphere

- To provide an opportunity to consider a teaching episode thoughtfully, analytically, and objectively

- To develop habits of reflective thought about teaching

- To provide for peer teaching

- To provide immediate feedback and reflection opportunities

- To provide an alternative teaching model

SOURCE: Adapted with permission from Cruickshank (1985).

Criteria for using the reflective teaching strategy are few (Cruickshank, 1985). The lesson must be of high interest to the practitioner. Reflective teaching lessons focus on one of three domains: cognitive, psychomotor, or affective. Lessons are brief, taking no more than 15 minutes. They are self-contained and use a minimum of materials. Objectives for the lessons must be measurable.

There are numerous benefits to reflective teaching (see Table 5.2). Reflective teaching

- Provides a nonthreatening environment in which to practice
- Allows experimentation and sharing of teaching experiences
- Provides an atmosphere that promotes peer communication
- Fosters self-review and peer review of teaching skills
- Provides an opportunity to observe others
- Encourages practitioners to value practical knowledge
- Improves articulation of knowledge
- Develops collegiality
- Makes for efficient use of time and money in providing teaching practice
- Provides practitioners with immediate feedback on teaching performance
- Focuses or refocuses on insights into teaching

**Table 5.2**     Reflective Teaching Benefits

- Provides a nonthreatening environment

- Allows experimentation and sharing of teaching experiences

- Promotes peer communication

- Fosters self-review and peer review of teaching skills

- Allows opportunity to observe others

- Allows practitioners to come to value practical knowledge

- Improves articulation of knowledge

- Develops collegiality

- Makes for efficient use of time and money in providing teaching practice

- Provides practitioners with immediate feedback on teaching performance

- Focuses on insights into teaching

SOURCE: Adapted with permission from Cruickshank (1985).

# REFLECTIVE ACTIVITIES

## Technical

At a technical level, practitioners will be using Cruickshank's (1985) reflective teaching format to prepare and teach a lesson. Task 21, "The Anxiety Task," provides a teaching experience using the affective domain. Task 22, "Lines of Symmetry Task," is a reflective teaching experience using the cognitive domain. Both activities support the need for practitioners reflecting at a technical level to make references to past experiences; to practice meeting a specified objective in a risk-free environment; and to focus on particular behavior, content, or skills.

## Task 21    The Anxiety Task

*Topic:* Practicum strategies: Reflective teaching—Affective domain (adapted from Cruickshank, 1987)

*Objective:* The practitioner will teach a reflective teaching lesson and then be reviewed by peers in a discussion format.

*Materials:* Sufficient copies of The Anxiety Task (Table 5.3) for groups of four to six practitioners; overhead transparencies of Aims of Reflective Teaching (Table 5.1) and Reflective Teaching Benefits (Table 5.2)

*Time:* One 10-minute period; one 40-minute period

*Procedure:* Day 1

1. Divide practitioners into groups of four to six, with the tallest individual being designated as the teacher. All team members will teach a lesson using the model as time permits. (Other lessons at the affective, cognitive, and psychomotor levels may be found in Cruickshank's [1987] *Reflective Teaching: The Preparation of Students of Teaching.*)

2. Provide the practitioners with a brief background and the aims and benefits of reflective teaching by using overhead transparencies for each topic.

3. Distribute The Anxiety Task to the designated teachers, instructing them that they will be expected to review the lesson and then teach the lesson to the remaining team members on Day 2. Each lesson consists of objectives, subject matter, materials, time limitations, and suggested guidelines. Concentration will be on the teaching process.

Day 2

1. Allow teaching time of no more than 15 minutes, which includes administration of the pretest and posttest.

2. At the end of the designated time period, instruct the designated teacher to give the Learner Satisfaction Forms to other team members and to compare the pretest and posttest evaluations. Allow 5 minutes.

3. The designated teacher will use the small-group reflection form to lead discussion among the team members on the process of the teaching episode. Recording reflections made should be done during this time period. All materials should be collected by the facilitator for review. Allow 10 minutes.

4. During the remaining 10 minutes, the facilitator should lead the whole group in discussion of the debriefing questions.

5. On subsequent days, repeat the process so that all team members have a chance to become designated teachers.

*Evaluation:* The practitioners taught a reflective teaching lesson, followed by a peer review of the designated teacher using a discussion format.

*Debriefing:* 1. In what various ways did the designated practitioners teach the reflective teaching lesson?

2. How successful was the methodology in bringing about learner satisfaction and achievement?

3. What happened to facilitate learning and satisfaction?

4. What, if anything, could be changed to increase learner achievement and satisfaction?

5. What was learned (or rediscovered) about teaching or learning that may be worth reflecting on for later use?

6. To what extent was the designated teacher satisfied or dissatisfied with the teaching or learning, and why?

**Table 5.3**    Reflective Teaching Task: Affective Domain

Designated Teachers    _____

Group Members          _____

_____

_____

_____

## THE ANXIETY TASK

### Description of Your Reflective Thinking Task

You are to teach this short lesson to a small group of your peers. The exercise is intended to provide an opportunity to experience teaching and then to reflect on the shared teaching-learning experience. Plan to teach it in such a way that you believe both learning and satisfaction will result.

Your lesson will be taught on _____ (date).

### Introduction to the Lesson

Teachers foster attitude change—that is, they attempt to get students to change their minds about people, events, content to be learned, and so on. The following are examples of teachers fostering attitude change:

1. A social studies teacher engages the class in a discussion of the contributions of persons of a variety of national origins to present-day American culture.

2. A foreign language teacher shows the class how learning a foreign language will be helpful in their everyday life.

3. A home economics teacher encourages boys to consider performing home tasks associated with assuming family responsibility.

Following is a goal that requires you to foster attitude change with a small group of your peers. The task was selected because your success in accomplishing it probably will not be dependent on your knowledge of some academic subject or previous experience you might have had.

SOURCE: Adapted with permission from Cruickshank (1985).

*(Continued)*

## Your Goal

Your goal is to get as many of your learners as possible to change their attitudes toward the notion of anxiety. Specifically, you should try to get your learners to disagree with the following statements:

Anxiety breeds anxiety.

Anxiety increases performance.

Anxiety stems from lack of preparation.

Anxiety is a learned attitude.

You will have no more than 15 minutes in which to accomplish your goal.

## Materials

1. Pretest
2. Posttest
3. Scoring Sheet
4. Learner Satisfaction Forms
5. Group follow-up discussion questions

## Special Conditions and Limitations

Before you begin teaching, obtain a copy of the pretest for each learner. Distribute the pretests and have learners respond to them. Collect the pretests before you start.

## Ending the Lesson

Give your learners the posttest, and when they are finished (no more than 2 minutes), return their pretests and ask them to indicate any changes that they may have made from pretest to posttest. Next, distribute the Learner Satisfaction Forms. While they are being completed, collect the pretests and posttests and record the scores on the Scoring Sheet. Return the pretests and posttests and collect the Learner Satisfaction Forms.

Begin to work through the questions for small-group discussion with your learners. Record responses from your group on the form provided. Put the designated teacher's name and all group members' names on the top of page 1. Hand all materials to the instructor.

SOURCE: Adapted with permission from Cruickshank (1985).

*(Continued)*

**Table 5.3** (Continued)

## PRETEST FOR THE ANXIETY TASK

Name _____

Following are statements about anxiety. Rate each on the basis of whether you agree or disagree with it by placing a check mark in one column after each statement. The check mark must be in a box and not on a line.

| Statements | Strongly agree | Agree | Disagree | Strongly disagree |
|---|---|---|---|---|
| 1. Anxiety breeds anxiety. | | | | |
| 2. Anxiety increases performance. | | | | |
| 3. Anxiety stems from lack of preparation. | | | | |
| 4. Anxiety is a learned attitude. | | | | |

SOURCE: Adapted with permission from Cruickshank (1985).

*(Continued)*

**POSTTEST FOR THE ANXIETY TASK**

Name _____

## Part A

Following are statements about anxiety. Rate each on the basis of whether you agree or disagree with it by placing a check mark in one column after each statement. The check mark must be in a box and not on a line.

| Statements | Strongly agree | Agree | Disagree | Strongly disagree |
|---|---|---|---|---|
| 1. Anxiety breeds anxiety. | | | | |
| 2. Anxiety increases performance. | | | | |
| 3. Anxiety stems from lack of preparation. | | | | |
| 4. Anxiety is a learned attitude. | | | | |

## Part B

Do you think that your attitude toward anxiety has been modified somewhat by this reflective teaching experience? (Check one box)

_____ Yes

_____ No

SOURCE: Adapted with permission from Cruickshank (1985).

*(Continued)*

**Table 5.3** (Continued)

## SCORING SHEET FOR THE ANXIETY TASK

Once your learners have completed both the pretest and the posttest, you can count how many of them changed or did not change their attitudes toward each statement in the desired direction.

Note: Each row (across) in the scoring box will total your number of learners.

| Statements | Number of learners who changed their attitudes in the desired direction | Number of learners who did not change their attitudes in the desired direction |
|---|---|---|
| 1. Anxiety breeds anxiety. | | |
| 2. Anxiety increases performance. | | |
| 3. Anxiety stems from lack of preparation. | | |
| 4. Anxiety is a learned attitude. | | |
| Total (add down) | | |

## Part B

How many of your learners felt their attitudes toward anxiety were moderated from this experience? _____

SOURCE: Adapted with permission from Cruickshank (1985).

## SMALL-GROUP DISCUSSION QUESTIONS
## FOR THE REFLECTIVE TEACHING TASK

1. What probably influenced the way this lesson was taught the most: the content, the learners, the context or setting, the teacher's views of and experiences with teaching, available materials, or other? How did these factors affect how the lesson was taught?

2. Given the posttest results, to what extent did learners learn?

3. Based on the comments made on the Learner Satisfaction Forms, to what extent did instruction result in satisfaction?

4. What does the group believe contributed most to achievement and satisfaction?

5. What does the group believe got in the way of achievement and satisfaction?

6. What did you learn or recall about effective teaching and learning? Enumerate at least two insights.

7. How do you feel about this teaching-learning experience?

SOURCE: Adapted with permission from Cruickshank (1985).

*(Continued)*

**Table 5.3** (Continued)

## LEARNER SATISFACTION FORM
## FOR THE REFLECTIVE TEACHING LESSON

Name _____

1. During the lesson, how satisfied were you as a learner?

   _____ Very satisfied

   _____ Satisfied

   _____ Unsatisfied

   _____ Very unsatisfied

2. Suggest anything and everything that could have been done to increase your satisfaction with the topic, the teaching, or achievement. Be as analytical and critical (in the best sense) as you possibly can. Your responsibility is to make the teacher think deeply about teaching and learning.

## LEARNER SATISFACTION FORM
## FOR THE REFLECTIVE TEACHING LESSON

Name _____

1. During the lesson, how satisfied were you as a learner?

   _____ Very satisfied

   _____ Satisfied

   _____ Unsatisfied

   _____ Very unsatisfied

2. Suggest anything and everything that could have been done to increase your satisfaction with the topic, the teaching, or achievement. Be as analytical and critical (in the best sense) as you possibly can. Your responsibility is to make the teacher think deeply about teaching and learning.

SOURCE: Adapted with permission from Cruickshank (1985).

## Task 22    Lines of Symmetry Task

*Topic:* Practicum strategies: Reflective teaching—Affective domain (adapted from Cruickshank, 1987)

*Objective:* The practitioner will teach a reflective teaching lesson and then be reviewed by peers in a discussion format.

*Materials:* Copies of Reflective Teaching Task: Cognitive Domain (Table 5.4) for groups of four to six practitioners; clear transparencies of Aims of Reflective Teaching (Table 5.1) and Reflective Teaching Benefits (Table 5.2)

*Time:* One 10-minute period; one 40-minute period

*Procedure:* **Day 1**

1. Divide practitioners into groups of four to six, with the tallest individual being designated as the teacher. All team members will teach a lesson using the model as time permits. (Other lessons at the affective, cognitive, and psychomotor levels may be found in Cruickshank's [1987] *Reflective Teaching: The Preparation of Students of Teaching.*)

2. Provide the practitioners with a brief background and the aims and benefits of reflective teaching by using the overhead transparencies for each topic.

3. Distribute the Lines of Symmetry Task to the designated teachers, instructing them that they will be expected to review the lesson and then teach the lesson to the remaining team members on Day 2. Each lesson consists of objectives, subject matter, materials, time limitations, and suggested guidelines. Concentration will be on the teaching process.

**Day 2**

1. Allow teaching time of no more than 15 minutes, which includes administration of the pretest and posttest.

2. At the end of the designated time period, instruct the designated teacher to give the Learner Satisfaction Forms to other team members and to compare the pretest and posttest evaluations. Allow 5 minutes.

3. The designated teacher will use the small-group reflection form to lead discussion among the team members on the process of the teaching episode. Reflections should be recorded during this time period. All materials should be collected by the facilitator for review. Allow 10 minutes.

4. During the remaining 10 minutes, the facilitator should lead the whole group in discussion of the debriefing questions.

5. On subsequent days, repeat the process so that all team members have a chance to become designated teachers.

*Evaluation:* The practitioners each taught a reflective teaching lesson, followed by a peer review of the designated teacher using a discussion format.

*Debriefing:*

1. In what various ways did the designated practitioners teach the reflective teaching lesson?

2. How successful was the methodology in bringing about learner satisfaction and achievement?

3. What happened to facilitate learning and satisfaction?

4. What, if anything, could be changed to increase learner achievement and satisfaction?

5. What was learned (or rediscovered) about teaching or learning that may be worth reflecting on for later use?

6. To what extent was the designated teacher satisfied or dissatisfied with the teaching or learning, and why?

**Table 5.4**    Reflective Teaching Task: Cognitive Domain

Designated Teachers    _____

Group Members    _____

_____

_____

_____

## LINES OF SYMMETRY TASK

### Description of Your Reflective Thinking Task

You are to teach this short lesson to a small group of your peers. The exercise is intended to provide an opportunity to experience teaching and then to reflect on the shared teaching-learning experience. Plan to teach it in such a way that you believe both learning and satisfaction will result.

Your lesson will be taught on _____ (date).

### Introduction to the Lesson

Teachers foster cognitive change—that is, they attempt to get students to add concepts to their existing schemata. The following are examples of teachers fostering cognitive change:

1. An elementary teacher describes how to perform addition and demonstrates by example.

2. A dance teacher describes how to do a step and demonstrates by example.

3. A chemistry teacher describes how to light a burner and demonstrates by example.

4. A physical education teacher describes how to do a flip and demonstrates by example.

The following goal is one that requires you to foster cognitive change with a small group of your peers. The task was selected because your success in accomplishing it probably will not be dependent on your knowledge of some academic subject or previous experience you might have had.

SOURCE: Adapted with permission from Cruickshank (1985).

*(Continued)*

**Table 5.4** (Continued)

## Your Goal

Your goal is to get as many of your learners as possible to be able to correctly identify the lines of symmetry of a square, a triangle, and the letters in their names. You will have 15 minutes in which to accomplish your objective.

Symmetry involves the use of a line or lines that promote balance or a point about which a figure or design is rotated. It requires equity of parts. The line of symmetry for a capital A is drawn vertically through the center of the letter. In contrast, a circle has an infinite number of lines of symmetry.

## Materials

1. Pretest

2. Posttest

3. Scoring Sheet

4. Learner Satisfaction Forms

5. Small-group follow-up discussion questions

## Special Conditions and Limitations

Before you begin teaching, obtain a copy of the pretest for each learner. Distribute the pretests and have learners respond to them. Collect the pretests before you start.

## Ending the Lesson

Distribute copies of the posttest. When they are finished (no more than 2 minutes), return their pretests and ask them to indicate any changes that they may have made from pretest to posttest. Next, distribute the Learner Satisfaction Forms, and while they are being completed, collect the pretests and posttests and record the scores in the box on the Scoring Sheet. Return the pre- and posttests and collect the Learner Satisfaction Forms.

Begin to work through the questions for small-group discussion with your learners. Record responses from your group on the form provided. Put designated teacher's name and all group members' names on the top of page 1. Hand all materials to the instructor.

SOURCE: Adapted with permission from Cruickshank (1985).

**PRETEST FOR THE LINES OF SYMMETRY TASK**

Name _____

Identify the lines of symmetry for the following figures:

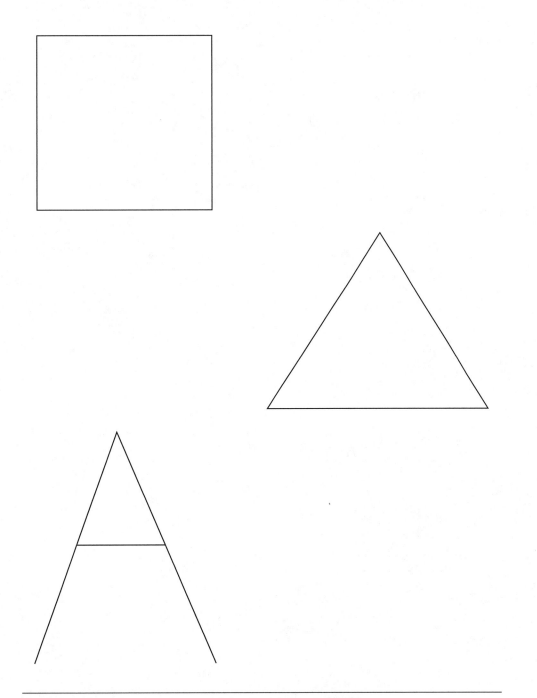

SOURCE: Adapted with permission from Cruickshank (1985).

*(Continued)*

**Table 5.4** (Continued)

## POSTTEST FOR THE LINES OF SYMMETRY TASK

Name _____

Identify the lines of symmetry for the following figures:

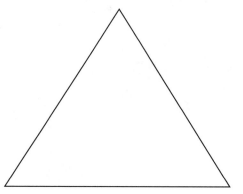

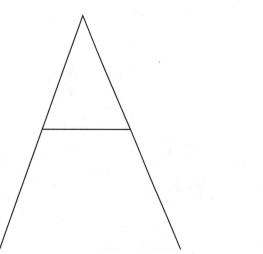

SOURCE: Adapted with permission from Cruickshank (1985).

## SCORING SHEET FOR THE LINES OF SYMMETRY TASK

Once your learners have completed both the pretest and the posttest, you can count how many of them were able to learn the placement of the lines of symmetry in the square, the triangle, and the letters of their names. Tally the correct responses for each test.

|  | *Pretest* | *Posttest* |
|---|---|---|
| Square |  |  |
| Triangle |  |  |
| Letters |  |  |

SOURCE: Adapted with permission from Cruickshank (1985).

*(Continued)*

**Table 5.4** (Continued)

## SMALL-GROUP DISCUSSION QUESTIONS
## FOR THE REFLECTIVE TEACHING LESSON

1. What was probably the strongest influence on the way this lesson was taught: the content, the learners, the context or setting, the teacher's views of and experiences with teaching, available materials, or other? How did these factors probably affect how the lesson was taught?

2. Given the posttest results, to what extent did learners learn?

3. Based on the comments made on the Learner Satisfaction Forms, to what extent did instruction result in satisfaction?

4. What does the group believe contributed most to achievement and satisfaction?

5. What does the group believe got in the way of achievement and satisfaction?

6. What did you learn or recall about effective teaching and learning? Enumerate at least two insights.

7. How do you feel about the teaching-learning experience?

SOURCE: Adapted with permission from Cruickshank (1985).

## LEARNER SATISFACTION FORM
## FOR THE REFLECTIVE TEACHING LESSON

Name _____

1. During the lesson, how satisfied were you as a learner?

   _____ Very satisfied

   _____ Satisfied

   _____ Unsatisfied

   _____ Very unsatisfied

2. Suggest anything and everything that could have been done to increase your satisfaction with the topic, the teaching, or achievement. Be as analytical and critical (in the best sense) as you possibly can. Your responsibility is to make the teacher think deeply about teaching and learning.

## LEARNER SATISFACTION FORM
## FOR THE REFLECTIVE TEACHING LESSON

Name _____

1. During the lesson, how satisfied were you as a learner?

   _____ Very satisfied

   _____ Satisfied

   _____ Unsatisfied

   _____ Very unsatisfied

2. Suggest anything and everything that could have been done to increase your satisfaction with the topic, the teaching, or achievement. Be as analytical and critical (in the best sense) as you possibly can. Your responsibility is to make the teacher think deeply about teaching and learning.

SOURCE: Adapted with permission from Cruickshank (1985).

*(Continued)*

## Contextual

Practitioners functioning at a contextual level look at alternative practices relative to the context of the situation. It is important to reflect upon educational theory and one's personal values when analyzing, clarifying, and validating contextual situations. The tasks at the contextual level support improvement of one's teaching in two ways. First, a rubric will be constructed based on values and interpretations of effective teaching. The second task allows the practitioner to use the rubric to self-evaluate and to evaluate peer microteaching.

## Task 23    Effective Teaching Rubric

*Topic:* Practicum strategies: Microteaching

*Objective:* The practitioner will determine effective teaching from past experiences in schooling, and then create a rubric to judge a microteaching experience.

*Materials:* Clear transparencies; individual copies of the Problem-Solving Scenario (Table 5.5); Problem-Solving Rubrics (Table 5.6); Definition of Rubric (Table 5.7); Sample Microteaching Rubric (Table 5.8)—optional; chart paper; markers

*Time:* 1 hour

*Procedure:*  1. Inform practitioners that they will be taking a test. The test is open-ended and should be answered to the best of their abilities within a 5-minute time frame. Distribute the Problem-Solving Scenario. Allow 10 minutes.

2. Using the Problem-Solving Rubrics transparency, have practitioners analyze a peer's answer to the problem. Discuss how well practitioners used each of the three rubrics. Ask what might have made the task easier to do (e.g., having success indicators beforehand). Using the Definition of Rubric transparency, discuss definition.

3. Knowing the criteria of success prior to microteaching is important. To develop the criteria, solicit observable indicators of effective teaching through a whole-group brainstorming activity. Write a list on chart paper as suggestions are given.

4. Once indicators have been listed, allow thorough discussion, making additions to or deletions from the list.

5. Using a clear transparency, begin construction of the rubric. Use a scale of 0 to 5, with 0 representing *no presentation* and 5 representing *top performance*. Solicit input from practitioners on key behaviors from the effective teaching list on which they would like their microteaching experience to be judged. Begin with Level-5 behaviors. List observable behaviors desired for an excellent teaching performance. An example of a completed rubric is included as an optional tool (see Table 5.6).

6. Use the same list of effective teaching behaviors when selecting those that indicate a 3 level. Then list the 1 level of behaviors. Indicators at Level 3 should reflect moderate teaching effectiveness. Indicators at a Level 1 reflect low teaching effectiveness.

7. Practitioners will use the rubric as self-evaluation and peer evaluation of microteaching experiences (such as in Task 24).

*Evaluation:* Practitioners collaborated to produce a rubric to be used in a microteaching situation.

*Debriefing:*  1. On what premise were your ideas of effective reaching based?

2. How did you feel after taking the problem-solving test, then finding out the criteria?

3. What are some of the benefits to using a rubric?

4. How might the microteaching rubric be amended?

5. What are other uses for such a rubric?

---

NOTE: The solution to the Problem-Solving Scenario is that Bill and Mary are cousins.

**Table 5.5**      Problem-Solving Scenario

Solve the following problem by working through a problem-solving strategy. Explain the method you used by writing your problem-solving process below the problem.

> Bill said to Tim, "You are my father." Tim said to Pat, "You are my mother." Pat said to Luke, "You are my son." Luke said to Mary, "You are my daughter." What is the relationship between Bill and Mary?

*Process:*

Copyright © 2005 by Corwin Press. All rights reserved. Reprinted from *Promoting Reflective Thinking in Teachers: 50 Action Strategies,* by Germaine L. Taggart and Alfred P. Wilson. Thousand Oaks, CA: Corwin Press, www.corwinpress.com. Reproduction authorized only for the local school site or nonprofit organization that has purchased this book.

**Table 5.6**    Problem-Solving Rubrics

*Handwriting and Neatness*

5   Well-formed letters and numbers, uniform slant, and no
    visible erasures

3   Fairly easy to read, letter formations lack consistency

1   Barely legible

*Creative Labels*

5   Labels are attention getting, unique, thought provoking, and
    imaginative

3   For the most part, representations are understandable

1   Label? What label?

*Number of Words*

5   More than 120 words are used in presenting solution
    (numbers with more than two digits constitute one word)

3   Fifty to 100 words are used in the explanation

1   One to 60 words are used (count single-digit numbers)

Copyright © 2005 by Corwin Press. All rights reserved. Reprinted from *Promoting Reflective Thinking in Teachers: 50 Action Strategies,* by Germaine L. Taggart and Alfred P. Wilson. Thousand Oaks, CA: Corwin Press, www.corwinpress.com. Reproduction authorized only for the local school site or nonprofit organization that has purchased this book.

**Table 5.7**    Definition of Rubric

# An assessment tool that provides standard criteria used in evaluating an action.

Copyright © 2005 by Corwin Press. All rights reserved. Reprinted from *Promoting Reflective Thinking in Teachers: 50 Action Strategies,* by Germaine L. Taggart and Alfred P. Wilson. Thousand Oaks, CA: Corwin Press, www.corwinpress.com. Reproduction authorized only for the local school site or nonprofit organization that has purchased this book.

**Table 5.8**   Sample Microteaching Rubric

5   Uses eye contact
Lesson has clarity (flow, accurate knowledge, clear directions)
Voice is clear, articulate, and uses good grammar
Interacts with students positively
Is organized and prepared
Communicates at instructional level
Uses appropriate facial expressions and body language
Relates purpose; brings about closure
Lesson is varied and attention getting
Uses materials appropriately
Uses high-level questioning
Checks for understanding
Dresses professionally
Moves around the room

3   Occasionally makes eye contact
Has some flaws in lesson delivery
Poor grammar, articulation, or clarity of voice is occasionally evident
Occasionally interacts with students or has occasional negative interaction
Loses place in lesson; is somewhat disorganized
Communicates at instructional level for most of lesson
Facial expressions and body language are generally open and accepting
Purpose and closure are weakly related
Uses attention-getting and varied strategies sometimes ineffectively
Materials and high-level questioning used appropriately most of the time
Randomly checks for understanding
Dresses unprofessionally
Somewhat mobile in presentation

1   Seldom uses eye contact or interacts with students
Lesson lacks clarity
Voice lacks clarity; uses poor grammar or articulation or both
Lacks organization; seems unprepared
Unsure of instructional level
Facial expression and body language are unwelcoming
Purpose is unclear or missing; closure is missing
Lesson lacks variety and is not attention getting
Materials used inappropriately; only low-level questions asked
Does not check for understanding
Dress is inappropriate
Does not move around the room

0   No presentation

Copyright © 2005 by Corwin Press. All rights reserved. Reprinted from *Promoting Reflective Thinking in Teachers: 50 Action Strategies,* by Germaine L. Taggart and Alfred P. Wilson. Thousand Oaks, CA: Corwin Press, www.corwinpress.com. Reproduction authorized only for the local school site or nonprofit organization that has purchased this book.

| *Task 24* | **Effective Teaching to Peers** |

*Topic:* Practicum strategies: Microteaching

*Objective:* The practitioner will prepare and teach a lesson to peers. Facilitator-, peer-, and self-evaluation using a rubric will be used to assess the outcome of effective teaching.

*Materials:* Camcorder; VHS cassette tape; TV-VCR; microteaching rubric (from Task 23); individual copies of the Lesson Plan Format (Table 5.9)

*Time:* One 50-minute period; one 15-minute microteaching period; one 30-minute review session

*Procedure:* Day 1

1. During whole-group discussion, inform practitioners that they will prepare a microteaching lesson for teaching. The practitioner first decides the topic or process to teach and then prepares a plan of the lesson. The format of the lesson is preestablished. Distribute the Lesson Plan Format. Using the Lesson Plan Format, present the overall format of the lesson. A title for the lesson will be specified, as well as the topic around which the lesson will be built. For example, in mathematics, the topics may pertain to the process standard of problem solving and the product standard of measurement. Specific observable performance objectives are specified on the plan. Objectives should inform the reader of what the students will learn, how they will demonstrate that learning has taken place, and by what criteria the learning will be measured. Materials needed, time constraints, and prerequisite skills needed prior to teaching are listed. A procedure for teaching the lesson should be outlined in detail, preferably through a number system for ease of reference. Included in the teaching procedure are an introduction, a review, and a strategy development. A conclusion and evaluation of the lesson's effectiveness in producing the desired objective ends the lesson. Extensions in the form of enrichment, reteaching, or special adaptations for the student learners are drafted and resources are listed for future reference.

2. Ask for any clarifying questions. Assign a schedule of microteaching times for each practitioner.

3. The practitioner prepares and rehearses the lesson and prepares two copies of the plan: one to refer to while teaching and the other for the facilitator or peer.

Day 2

1. The practitioner teaches the lesson during a preset time period. During the teaching experience, the facilitator assesses the microteaching. Using a copy of the plan, make written comments on the effectiveness of the plan in covering the objective, its portability, and the implementation of the plan by the practitioner. Be positive regarding strategies and concepts effectively used. Note improvements needed in a constructive manner.

2. Prior to the microteaching lesson, select one to four peers to perform an assessment of the practitioner teaching. Both the facilitator and peer reviewers should rate the practitioner using the microteaching rubric (Task 23) prepared by the group prior to the microteaching experience.

3. During the course of the microteaching, have the lesson videotaped by a peer or technician. The goal of videotaping is to capture the interaction of the classroom.

4. The videotaped lesson is to be reviewed by the practitioner between the teaching experience and an assigned review time with the facilitator. The practitioners use the rubric for microteaching to critique their own lessons. This review should be accomplished soon after the microteaching event.

*Day 3*

1. The tape and critique of the practitioner are reviewed together by the facilitator and practitioner. The practitioner explains his or her critique using the rubric, the video is viewed with comments made by either the practitioner or the facilitator, and the lesson plan with facilitator comments and peer critiques is given to the practitioner. At this time, a final grade determination is made, if needed, and goals are established for the next microteaching task.

*Evaluation:* Practitioners planned, implemented, and evaluated a microteaching lesson.

*Debriefing:* 1. What parts of the microteaching experience went well? What parts needed improvement?

2. What will be your goal for improvement in your next teaching experience?

3. What are some of the benefits to using a rubric?

4. What are some of the benefits of performing a microteaching lesson?

5. How is teaching to peers different than teaching to younger students?

**Table 5.9**    Lesson Plan Format

I.  Teacher Information

Title of lesson

Topic(s)

Student level

Standards

Teacher background information

Objectives

II.  Teaching Procedures

Introduction

Review

Strategies

Conclusion

Evaluation

III.  Extensions

IV.  Reteaching activities

V.  Resources

Copyright © 2005 by Corwin Press. All rights reserved. Reprinted from *Promoting Reflective Thinking in Teachers: 50 Action Strategies,* by Germaine L. Taggart and Alfred P. Wilson. Thousand Oaks, CA: Corwin Press, www.corwinpress.com. Reproduction authorized only for the local school site or nonprofit organization that has purchased this book.

## Dialectical

Practicum strategies at the dialectical level deal with critical examination of underlying assumptions, norms, and rules. Social consequences are explored and choices are made after reviewing internal and external aspects of a situation. Examinations of contradictions and systematic attempts to resolve issues are characteristics of practitioners functioning in the dialectical mode. Practitioners may apply practicum strategies to improve teaching within an inclusionary setting and by teaching the concept of classroom management styles to peers.

## Task 25    Inclusion: Teaching Effectiveness

*Topic:*   Practicum strategies: Microteaching

*Objective:*   The practitioner will use a 30-minute videotaped recording of his or her teaching to assess teaching effectiveness with special needs children in an inclusionary setting.

*Materials:*   Camcorder; VHS cassette tape; TV-VCR; individual copies of the Inclusion Checklist (Table 5.10); transparency of Definition of Inclusion (Table 5.11); individual copies of the Inclusion Information Sheet (Table 5.12) and Lesson Plan Format (Table 5.9)

*Time:*   One 50-minute period; one 15-minute to 30-minute teaching period; one 40-minute peer review session

*Procedure:*   *Day 1*

1. Distribute Inclusion Checklist. Group practitioners by grade or age level of their field assignments. Buzz groups should have three to five practitioners per group for best results. Split larger groups into smaller ones. No single-practitioner groups are appropriate for this task.

2. Use the transparency of Definition of Inclusion to introduce the topic, then introduce and discuss the Inclusion Checklist. Allow 15 minutes for practitioners to complete the checklists individually, then discuss items on the checklist relative to their school community. A recorder (the person with the most children in the classroom) takes notes.

3. During whole-group discussion, have group leaders (practitioners with the most course work involving special needs children) report findings of buzz groups. Use Inclusion Information Sheet copies to assist you in discussing the issue.

4. Practitioners will return to teams formed during buzz groups. The object is to use the Lesson Plan Format to begin planning a 15- to 30-minute lesson for an inclusionary classroom. All major points considered in discussion should be accounted for.

5. Each team member is assigned to teach a videotaped lesson in his or her field setting. At least one peer will observe the teaching experience and critique it using the rubric from Task 23. Team members should work out a schedule for teaching and reviewing the microteaching lesson.

*Day 2*

After teaching the lesson, each practitioner will view the videotape with a team member. A constructive critique of the lesson plan delivery will be made using the Inclusion Checklist as a guide.

*Evaluation:*   Practitioners planned, implemented, evaluateded and videotaped lesson taught to students in an inclusionary classroom.

*Debriefing:*   Practitioners will answer debriefing questions using a dialogue journal.

1. What problems, if any, did I see in my classroom regarding the inclusion of special needs children?

2. What does inclusion mean in my classroom?

3. What solutions to the situation did I put into the lesson plan in an effort to resolve the problem(s)?

4. What factors affected the resolution of the problem(s)?

**Table 5.10**    Inclusion Checklist

Check the line at the right of each question if you would answer *yes* to it.

1. Do I demonstrate a genuine belief
   that all children are entitled
   to an equitable education?                        _____

2. Do I demonstrate a belief
   that all children can learn?                       _____

3. Is instruction individualized in
   my field setting for all children?                 _____

4. Do I adapt my teaching for
   special-needs children?                            _____

5. Are resources available to
   meet the needs of diverse
   populations of students?                           _____

6. Do I demonstrate skill in
   meeting the needs of all children?                 _____

7. Is my field setting a
   supportive environment?                            _____

8. Are special-needs children
   participating in my classroom
   to the fullest extent possible?                    _____

Copyright © 2005 by Corwin Press. All rights reserved. Reprinted from *Promoting Reflective Thinking in Teachers: 50 Action Strategies*, by Germaine L. Taggart and Alfred P. Wilson. Thousand Oaks, CA: Corwin Press, www.corwinpress.com. Reproduction authorized only for the local school site or nonprofit organization that has purchased this book.

**Table 5.11**  Definition of Inclusion

# A commitment to educate each child, to the maximum extent appropriate, in the school and classroom the child would normally attend.

Copyright © 2005 by Corwin Press. All rights reserved. Reprinted from *Promoting Reflective Thinking in Teachers: 50 Action Strategies*, by Germaine L. Taggart and Alfred P. Wilson. Thousand Oaks, CA: Corwin Press, www.corwinpress.com. Reproduction authorized only for the local school site or nonprofit organization that has purchased this book.

**Table 5.12**    Inclusion Information Sheet

The *Individuals with Disabilities Education Act* of 1990 (IDEA), formerly the *Education for All Handicapped Children Act* of 1975, stipulates that children with disabilities must be provided a free and appropriate public education in the least restrictive environment. *Least restrictive environment* generally means that children with disabilities are, to the maximum extent possible, educated with nondisabled children. Children may be placed in special classes or facilities only when the nature of their disabilities precludes satisfactory achievement in a regular classroom.

Inclusion, per se, is not mentioned in IDEA. Inclusion is a commitment to educate every child, to the maximum extent possible, in the school or classroom he or she would otherwise attend. Support services are brought to the child rather than moving the child to a segregated setting.

*Inclusion is*

- All children learning in the same supportive environment

- Individualization to meet the needs of all children

- Equal participation by all children to the greatest extent possible

- Social relationships between students with and without disabilities

- Collaboration between regular and special education

- Support in the classroom setting for teachers and students

- All children understanding and accepting human differences

- Parents participating to the fullest extent possible in the education of their children

Copyright © 2005 by Corwin Press. All rights reserved. Reprinted from *Promoting Reflective Thinking in Teachers: 50 Action Strategies*, by Germaine L. Taggart and Alfred P. Wilson. Thousand Oaks, CA: Corwin Press, www.corwinpress.com. Reproduction authorized only for the local school site or nonprofit organization that has purchased this book.

### Task 26    Effective Teaching of Peers

*Topic:*    Practicum strategies: Microteaching

*Objective:*    The practitioner will prepare and teach a lesson to peers. Facilitator-, peer-, and self-evaluation using a rubric will be used to assess the effectiveness of the teaching.

*Materials:*    Camcorder; three VHS cassette tapes; three TV-VCRs; microteaching rubric (from Task 23); transparency of Definition of Classroom Management (Table 3.4); copies of Synopsis of Classroom Management Styles (Table 3.5); Lesson Plan Format (Table 5.9); clear transparencies; one or two decks of playing cards

*Time:*    One 90-minute period

*Procedure:*    1. Discuss with the whole group the definition of classroom management. Ask for factors that have helped to determine practitioners' management styles. List these as presented on a clear transparency.

2. Group participants into three teams by randomly distributing an ace, a king, or a queen playing card to each practitioner. Each team will become an expert on either low, moderate, or high teacher-control environments. Each expert group meets to discuss the characteristics and approaches to their corresponding environmental control topic. Distribute Synopsis of Classroom Management Styles for the expert groups to use as information and to prompt discussion of possible examples. Allow about 15 minutes.

3. Experts will prepare a 5- to 10-minute lesson using the Lesson Plan Format and the microteaching rubric (from Task 23) to teach the remainder of the whole group about the level of control discussed in the team session. Allow 20 minutes.

4. Bring the whole group together for the presentation of the three lessons, each of which will be videotaped. Select four practitioners to use the rubric to assess the presentation of each group simultaneously with the facilitator.

5. When all microteachings are completed, allow each expert group to view and critique the lesson they planned and presented, using the microteaching rubric.

6. Discuss the microteachings with the whole group.

*Evaluation:*    Practitioners planned, implemented, evaluated, and videotaped lesson to peers regarding environmental controls within a classroom.

*Debriefing:*    1. In which control level do you feel most comfortable? Why?

2. What was your comfort level in the peer teaching situation? Was it problematic for you?

3. How was the teaching strategy decided within the group? Was it effective?

4. How were problems resolved within the group?

5. What would have made the teaching task easier to accomplish?

6. How was reflection about the microteaching episode accomplished?

# REFLECTIVE QUESTIONS

1. The use of occasional videotaping of teaching in classrooms is recommended. What benefits do you see for the practice?

2. How could reflective teaching be raised above a technical level?

3. What is the place of rubric construction in your classroom field setting?

# ACTION ASSIGNMENTS

## Technical

1. Compare and contrast the presentation of the cognitive and affective reflective teaching lessons taught. Discuss feelings that were experienced before, during, and after teaching each lesson and the possible reasons for them. Discuss improvements made and those yet to be made. Discuss a plan for future reflective action.

2. Use a reflective teaching lesson from Cruickshank (1985) to teach a lesson in the psychomotor domain.

## Contextual

1. Challenge yourself to devise an alternative means of assessing microteaching experiences.

2. Plan, implement, and evaluate a cooperative learning lesson plan.

## Dialectical

1. Prepare and present a lesson on an innovative strategy you would like to incorporate into the field setting. Research should be done on the strategy as well as lesson preparation. The presentation may be made to peers, administrators, and board members, or at a conference.

2. Create and use a rubric to assess videotaped vignettes of practitioners using innovative strategies in a field setting. Discuss the vignettes, the strategy, and the rubric as an evaluation tool.

# SUGGESTION FOR SUCCESS

Review the rubric with practitioners after initial use and adjust if necessary.

# JOURNALING REFLECTIVE GROWTH

1. Compare and contrast growth experienced before and after the practicum experience.

2. Discuss plans for future use of practicum strategies for building confidence, reflective thinking ability, and expertise in teaching.

3. Discuss changes to the practicum experiences that would be more beneficial to you.

# 6

# Narrative Reflection

*Narrative studies provide us with different kinds of knowledge and different ways of representing it, and studies done within the field have the potential to bring new meaning to teacher education and to the continuous experiences of change, of growth and of professional development in a teacher's life.*

—Beattie (1995)

---

### *Chapter Objectives*

**The facilitator will**

- Assist practitioners in demonstrating proficiency with the narrative strategies
- Be able to assess growth in reflective thinking upon application of the strategies
- Analyze personal competencies of a strategy to assist practitioners in preparing an action plan that will foster personal reflection upon return to the classroom situation
- Facilitate maintenance of reflective journals to be used by practitioners for personal growth assessment and for peer assessment

---

Research supports the use of narrative, or story, for enhancing reflective thinking (Bullough & Gitlin, 2001; Hattan & Smith, 1995; Henderson, 2001; Sparks-Langer et al., 1991). Narrative writing portrays an ongoing series of events that befalls one or more people. The story line usually relates to some motive and leads to a consequence or solution. Stories can be written to describe, explain, or express. Important elements of story are the chaining of events in a logical sequence and the building of events around a theme, a problem, or a character, either individually or collectively. Narrative strategies used to promote reflective thinking by this author are autobiographical sketches, case studies, and the use of study circles.

## AUTOBIOGRAPHICAL SKETCHES

Autobiographical sketches are a narrative strategy used frequently by teacher educators to prompt practitioners to look into their past to uncover preconceived theories about teaching and learning. The perspective of education brought out in the practitioner's story line is based on beliefs, intentions, interpretations, and interactions of a lifetime. An autobiographical frame of reference assists practitioners in making sense of current experiences and in responding rationally to stimuli within those experiences. Olson (1988) maintains that practitioners' actions reflect their culture and that autobiographies of practitioners represent, influence, and are influenced by the cultural context in which they live. Autobiographies also heighten practitioners' awareness of their own learning, allowing them to reflect on changing ideas and attitudes throughout their careers (Solas, 1992). In addition, use of autobiographical sketches

- Enhances qualitative research by opening new avenues of thought
- Provides a vehicle for curricula and educational reform
- Helps form the foundation for educational policy and practice
- Emancipates and empowers practitioners
- Promotes self-understanding, personal growth, and professional development

Writing autobiographies and then reflecting on the meaning and relevance of the story is a powerful tool for promoting professional growth. Holt-Reynolds (1991) writes that "biographical writing externalizes and makes accessible the interpretations . . . placed on . . . experiences; it invites [practitioners] to reveal the underpinnings for their belief systems, goals, and arguments about 'good' teaching" (p. 16). Smith (1991) supports the use of autobiographical reflections and dialogue to break a cycle of teaching that may not be in keeping with current ideals of best practice.

## CASE STUDIES

Extensive research (Bullough, 1993; Harrington, 1995; Levin, 1995) supports the value of case studies in educating practitioners. A case study is a problem-centered story used to assist practitioners in focusing on problems and solutions for those situations. Because of the complexities of teaching and learning, the limited time for classroom observations, and the need to systematically look at particular episodes or aspects of teaching, case studies have become a norm in teacher education programs. Additional benefits (Boyce, King, & Harris, 1993; Kleinfeld, 1991; Shulman, 1992) to using case studies in teacher education are that they

- Bridge theory to practice
- Enable analysis of problems and development of solutions
- Help practitioners recognize the potential for multiple solutions
- Help in evaluating feasibility of alternatives and consequences of actions
- Promote critical reflection and problem solving
- Teach about dispositions and habits of teaching

The following guidelines (Silverman, Welty, & Lyon, 1992; Stivers, 1991) are used in writing case studies:

## Observations

- Observe as a participant or nonparticipant
- Use narrative to capture the emotional and physical environment
- Provide thick description of each timed observation
- Express observations with detail, not inferences

## Problem Selection/Development

- Base cases on observations
- Make cases sound realistic
- Make the situation generalizable
- Interweave elements of the case to produce complex themes
- Choose problems with multiple solutions
- Make certain practitioners have the ability to resolve the problem

## Narrative Elements

The text of the case study should

- Be lively, fastpaced, and descriptive
- Use limited educational jargon
- Provide rich detail
- Engage the reader with a strong opening
- Include a climax or central incident
- Provide a gap between what is and what should be
- Present need for a decision by the practitioner
- Be organized in a logical manner
- Avoid stereotypical and biased language
- Be written in first or third person

## STUDY CIRCLES

By definition, study circles are a viable strategy for enhancing reflective thinking. Brevskolan (1980) defined the aim of study circles as

"greater understanding" or insight. Through their studies the members must be enabled to put their lives into perspective and to review their own subject in a wider context. . . . [They] must learn how to come to grips with problems and how to work out solutions in the situations that will confront them later on. (pp. 13–14)

Oliver (1987) supports the use of study circles in business and education. Study circles support democratic theory, foster self-growth through education, and enhance practitioners' sense of value to become intelligent participants. Oliver adds that study circles "move us toward a more just society . . . relate ideas to action, and . . . justify our rhetoric about civic and organizational activities" (p. 145).

According to Oliver (1987), essential components of study circles are

- Reliance on dialogue
- Equality and democracy among voluntary participants
- Empowerment of participants
- Collegiality
- Self-determination
- Time for continuity and conversation
- Active participation
- Group size: 5 to 20 participants
- Use of well-grounded study materials

## REFLECTIVE ACTIVITIES

### Technical

On a technical level, practitioners use past experiences as a frame of reference for making decisions regarding current practice. Behaviors, skills, and competencies have been developed primarily through observations during formal schooling experience. In the following tasks, practitioners will use existing schemata to create autobiographical sketches to access beliefs regarding teacher roles. Task 27 provides a case study for review by practitioners to augment existing schemata.

## Task 27    Using Case Study for Problem Resolution

*Topic:*  Narrative reflection: Case study

*Objective:*  The practitioner will analyze a case study to determine possible resolution to the problem posed.

*Materials:*  Definition of a Case Study (Table 6.1); individual copies of Case Study I (Table 6.2), Case Study II (Table 6.3), and Guidelines for Writing a Case Study (Table 6.4); clear transparencies

*Time:*  50 minutes

*Procedure:*  1. In a whole-group situation, present case study definition to practitioners. Explain that practitioners will be analyzing two case studies to determine possible solutions to problems. Distribute Case Study I. Allow practitioners time to silently read the case. Solicit possible solutions from practitioners and write them on a clear transparency. Stress that there can be multiple solutions and that all possible solutions are of value.

2. Randomly group practitioners into teams of three. Distribute Case Study II. The task for each team is to discuss all issues involved in the case to determine the best way to handle the problem. Allow 15 minutes.

3. Bring the whole group together for concluding discussion. Facilitator should solicit solutions from each team, write the solutions on a clear transparency, then facilitate the analysis of solutions and bridging of ideas presented.

4. Discuss the elements of a case study by asking practitioners for observed similarities between the formats of the two cases. Distribute and discuss Guidelines for Writing a Case Study.

*Evaluation:*  The practitioners determined possible solutions to a problem presented in case study format.

*Debriefing:*  1. How does the use of a case study follow the Reflective Thinking Model?

2. What were the bases for possible solutions presented?

3. Explain the similarities and differences in the resolution of the two problems.

4. Based on your response to Question 3, what are some guidelines to use when writing case studies?

**Table 6.1**    Definition of a Case Study

# A problem-centered story used to assist practitioners in focusing on problems and their solutions.

Copyright © 2005 by Corwin Press. All rights reserved. Reprinted from *Promoting Reflective Thinking in Teachers: 50 Action Strategies*, by Germaine L. Taggart and Alfred P. Wilson. Thousand Oaks, CA: Corwin Press, www.corwinpress.com. Reproduction authorized only for the local school site or nonprofit organization that has purchased this book.

**Table 6.2**     Case Study I

Ben is an 11-year-old boy in the fifth grade. He has a behavior disorder and a high anxiety level. He progresses well in Spanish and in art. However, he has a high frustration level when it comes to the main curriculum areas of science, mathematics, and social studies. He is off task most of the time and has increased difficulty in large groups. Ben takes medication before school and before he goes to physical education. Ben has frequent outbursts of "I don't understand!" followed by crying.

Ben's mother argues with him when he exhibits the yelling outburst that ends in crying at home. She never backs down or walks away from the outburst. His day at school is influenced by the way the day started out at home. The kind of day Ben will have is evident as soon as he walks through the door.

Mr. Ortiz is frequently interrupted by Ben during mathematics, social studies, and science:

"Mr. Ortiz, I don't understand what you are doing on that number line."

"Be patient, Ben, and I will explain it more in a minute."

"I don't understand!" Ben starts to cry.

Mr. Ortiz pays no attention to the crying and continues with the lesson. The crying stops within a few seconds.

After the lesson, Mr. Ortiz has the students pick partners and goes over to his desk while the students work in groups on problems covering the concept just taught. Ben sits at a desk with two other students but doesn't work with them. "Mr. Ortiz, they won't let me work with them!"

"Ben doesn't know what to do, and we don't want him in our group," is the reply from the group members.

What should Mr. Ortiz do? Should he go at a slower pace and hold up the other students? Should he require the other two to work with Ben and help him figure out the problems? Or is there another solution?

Copyright © 2005 by Corwin Press. All rights reserved. Reprinted from *Promoting Reflective Thinking in Teachers: 50 Action Strategies,* by Germaine L. Taggart and Alfred P. Wilson. Thousand Oaks, CA: Corwin Press, www.corwinpress.com. Reproduction authorized only for the local school site or nonprofit organization that has purchased this book.

**Table 6.3**     Case Study II

"Jake!"

"Andrew!"

The two captains picked their teams for recess. Over and over, names were called until there was only one boy left. As usual, it was Chris. He smiled and sat up eagerly in his chair until Luke called his name. Everyone could see that his presence made the teams uneven.

"Okay, who would like to be the umpire?" asked Ms. Smith.

Chris quickly raised his hand. No one else did.

"Chris, you can be the umpire, then."

The next week, when it was time to pick new teams, the situation was the same—Chris was the last person chosen. Again, he volunteered to be the umpire. Ms. Smith wondered why he was always picked last, but she wondered mostly why he kept smiling. She had never seen Chris upset about anything. He was a bolster of support to his classmates, but they gave him nothing in return. How could he continue to be so happy?

One day, another student, Cody, was having trouble with long division using decimals. When he was finished with his own work, Chris leaned over and carefully explained to Cody why the decimal needed to be moved and how the process worked. He then helped Cody until all the problems were finished and even made sure they were correct.

On another day, Ms. Smith had the students draw pictures of animals. Joe was frustrated because his bear "didn't look right." Chris turned to Joe, smiled, and said, "It's ok, Joe. Your bear doesn't have to look perfect. Just do your best."

On yet another day, Officer Martin came in to talk to the students about feelings and reactions people have to things that happen to them. One of his first examples was, "How would you feel if you were standing on the playground minding your own business when you suddenly felt a rock fly by your head?" While there were statements of "I'd beat 'em up!" and "I'd be mad!" Chris laughed and said, "Wow! I'd feel surprised!"

Chris's parents are presently going through a divorce. They won't speak to each other. The kids spend 3 days at Mom's, 4 days at Dad's, 4 days at Mom's, 3 days at Dad's, and so on. His father is dating other women who frequently spend the night. Chris never knows who will give him breakfast in the morning at his father's house.

Right now, the turmoil in Chris's life is not evident at school. He has never had top grades, just average. He simply smiles his ever-present smile and goes on. He seems very content with himself and who he is. Ms. Smith worries that he will be affected soon, and it may be worse than anyone would expect. What can she do to help Chris?

Copyright © 2005 by Corwin Press. All rights reserved. Reprinted from *Promoting Reflective Thinking in Teachers: 50 Action Strategies*, by Germaine L. Taggart and Alfred P. Wilson. Thousand Oaks, CA: Corwin Press, www.corwinpress.com. Reproduction authorized only for the local school site or nonprofit organization that has purchased this book.

**Table 6.4**     Guidelines for Writing a Case Study

*Observations*

Observe as a participant or nonparticipant

Use narrative to capture emotional and physical environments

Provide thick description of each timed observation

Express observations with detail, not inferences

*Problem selection/development*

Base cases on observations

Make cases sound realistic

Make the situation generalizable

Interweave elements of the case to produce complex themes

Make sure problematic situations have many possible solutions

Be certain that practitioners have the ability to resolve the problem

*Narrative elements*

Use lively, fast-paced, descriptive writing

Limit educational jargon

Provide rich detail

Engage the reader with a strong opening

Include a climax or central incident

Provide a gap between what is and what should be

Present need for a decision by major practitioner

Organize in a logical manner

Avoid stereotypical and biased language

Write in first or third person

SOURCE: Adapted from Silverman, Welty, and Lyon (1992); Stivers (1991).

| | |
|---|---|
| **Task 28** | **Using Autobiographical Sketches to Evaluate Beliefs Regarding Teacher Roles** |

*Topic:* Narrative reflection: Autobiographical sketches

*Objective:* The practitioner will determine the role of his or her past experiences and beliefs in determining existing perceptions of teacher roles.

*Materials:* Clear transparencies

*Time:* 40 minutes

*Procedure:* 1. Allow 20 minutes for practitioners to freely write autobiographical sketches on two or three incidents remembered from formal schooling. Explain that experiences would be more beneficial to later reflection if they were from episodes at various time periods.

2. When practitioners have finished writing, ask for roles of teachers based on episodes remembered during the freewriting exercise. A *role* is defined as a characteristic and expected social behavior of an individual. List roles as presented, on a clear transparency. Encourage practitioners to add supporting details to roles mentioned by relating personal experiences from autobiographical sketches. Discuss with practitioners the relevance of past experiences to personal perceptions.

*Evaluation:* Practitioners determined current perceptions of teacher roles through the use of autobiographical sketches.

*Debriefing:* 1. What value do you see in the use of autobiographical sketches?

2. In retrospect, what other incidents have helped to determine your perception of teacher roles?

3. How did you feel sharing your personal experiences with other practitioners?

4. What other areas of teaching might benefit from practitioner reflection using autobiographical sketches?

## Contextual

Practitioners functioning in the contextual mode make choices within their field settings based on knowledge and value commitments. In Task 29, practitioners will write a case study based on observations made in a field setting, then reflect on the problem inherent in the case. Using a study group approach in Task 30, practitioners will use story to analyze, clarify, and validate principles regarding effective classroom management.

| **Task 29** | **Writing a Case Study for Problem Resolution** |
|---|---|

*Topic:* Narrative reflection: Case study

*Objective:* The practitioner will observe a student in a classroom situation for 15 minutes a day on 3 separate days, then write a case study regarding an event indicative of the student's behavior.

*Materials:* Definition of a Case Study (Table 6.1); individual copies of Guidelines for Writing a Case Study (Table 6.4); clear transparencies

*Time:* One 50-minute period; three 15-minute observation periods; one 50-minute period

*Procedure:* **Day 1**

1. In a whole-group situation, present case study definition to practitioners. Explain that each practitioner will be observing a student in his or her respective field settings for 15 minutes on 3 different days to gather information for a case study of the student. Distribute Guidelines for Writing Case Studies and review the guidelines with practitioners. Practitioners are to write case studies based on information from their student observations using the guidelines discussed.

**Day 2**

1. With the whole group, discuss any experiences, positive or negative, that occurred during the observation or writing of the case studies.

2. Group practitioners in threes or fours by teaming them with individuals who have similar age- or grade-level field settings. No single-practitioner teams are allowed. Teams will review case studies presented.

3. The task for the practitioners will be to discuss the case studies written by each team member. Items to consider during the discussion are similarities and differences among the studies, benefits or detriments of using the guidelines, value of the case studies for future decisions in teaching, and possible solutions for each case. Teams should arbitrarily select a recorder and reporter. Allow 30 minutes.

4. In a whole-group situation, discuss the findings by asking the team reporters to explain what their team learned through using the case study strategy.

*Evaluation:* The practitioners determined possible solutions to problems presented in case studies written from observations in personal field settings.

*Debriefing:* 1. How does the use of a case study follow the Reflective Thinking Model (Figure 1.2)?

2. What were the bases for possible solutions presented?

3. What were the similarities and differences among the studies?

4. What may be the benefits or detriments of using the guidelines for writing case studies?

5. What value do case studies have for future decisions in teaching?

## *Task 30*  The Three Pigs, the Wolf, and Effective Teaching

*Topic:* Narrative reflection: Study circles

*Objective:* Using *The True Story of the 3 Little Pigs!*, by Scieszka (1989), as a catalyst, practitioners will delineate among ideas of effective classroom management by designating them to be of straw, stick, or brick value.

*Materials:* *The True Story of the 3 Little Pigs!* by J. Scieszka (1989); cutouts (enough for 10 of each per practitioner) of the straw, stick, and brick images (Figures 6.1A, 6.1B, 6.1C); masking tape or sticky tack; markers; labels placed on the wall about the room: *Straw, Sticks,* and *Bricks.*

*Time:* 50 minutes

*Procedure:* 1. Read *The True Story of the 3 Little Pigs!* to practitioners. Briefly discuss the implications of the pigs' use of straw, sticks, and bricks to build their houses.

2. Instruct practitioners to individually analyze their own classroom management strategies or those of teachers in classrooms in which they have observed. Reflect on those strategies in terms of effectiveness at keeping students on task within the context of a given situation.

3. Using the straw, sticks, and bricks cutouts, categorize the strategies according to effectiveness: least effective (straw), moderately effective (sticks), or highly effective (bricks). Write the strategies on the corresponding figures and place them on the wall under the appropriate category of effectiveness. Allow 15 minutes.

4. Refer practitioners to the strategy wall. Beginning with the least effective strategies, moving to those that are moderately effective, and last to those that are highly effective, encourage practitioners to comment on why strategies were placed in a particular category.

*Evaluation:* Practitioners placed classroom management strategies, either practiced or observed, into categories ranging from least effective to highly effective.

*Debriefing:* 1. What was one basis for your decisions on effectiveness of classroom management strategies?

2. How did discussion of the story prompt reflection on current classroom management strategies?

3. What additional educational topics may be reflected upon using study circles?

**Figure 6.1A** Material Cutouts: Straw

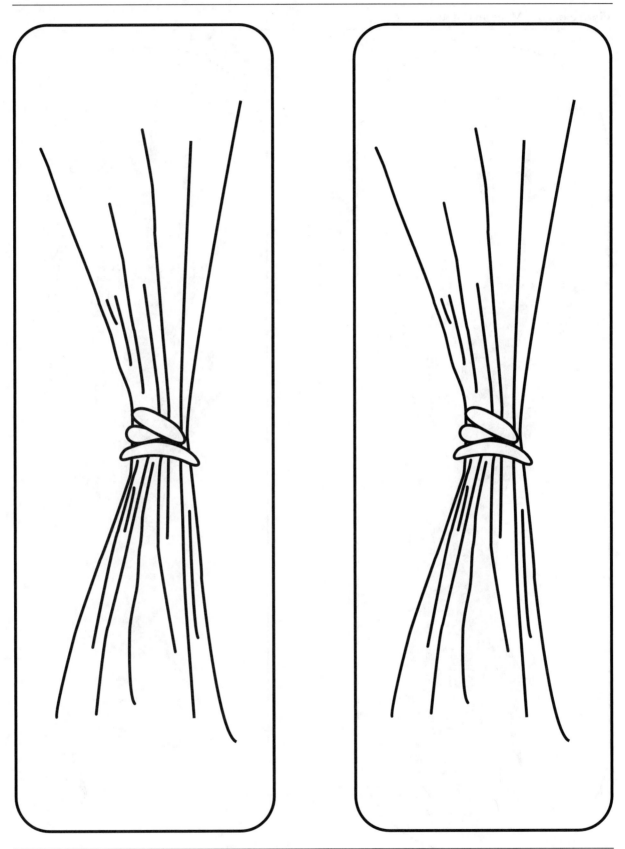

**Figure 6.1B**    Material Cutouts: Sticks

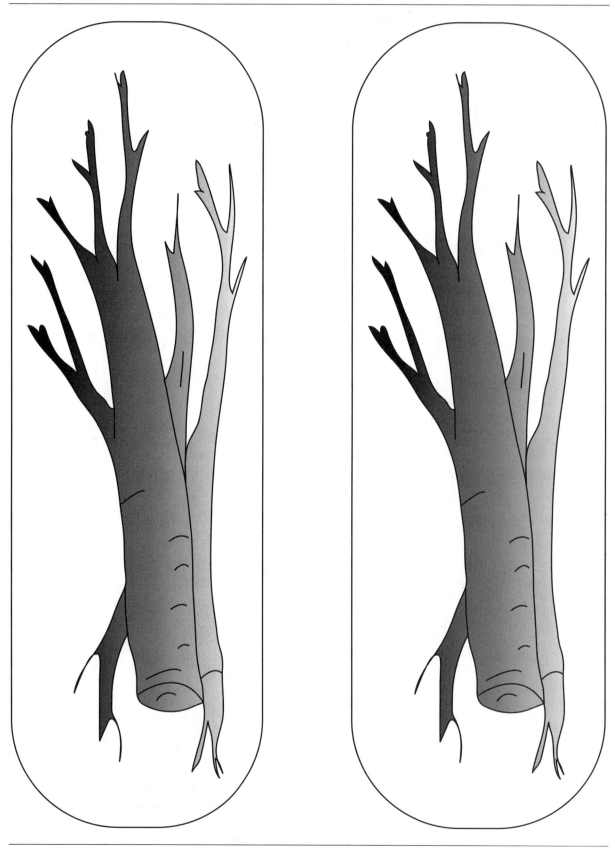

**Figure 6.1C** Material Cutouts: Bricks

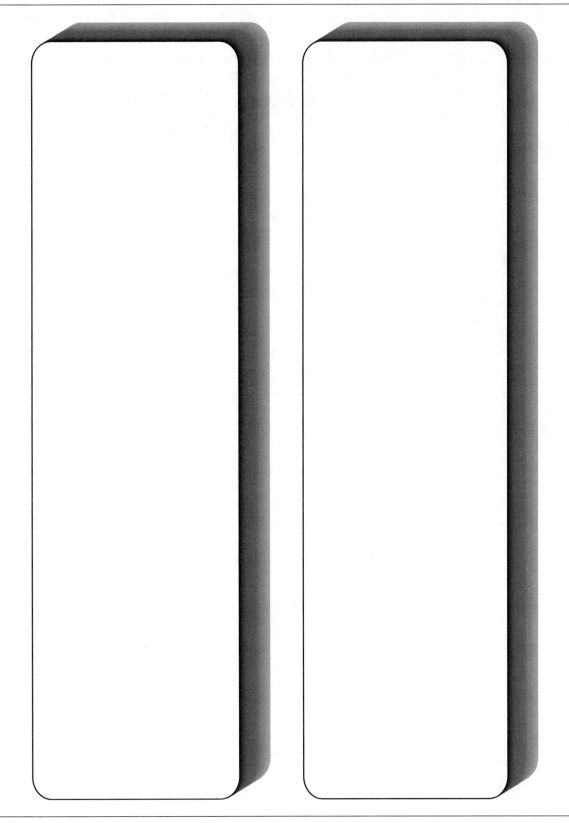

## Dialectical

The implications of educational practices found in Kidder's (1989) book *Among School Children* are far-reaching. In Task 31, the dialectical practitioner has an opportunity to review a synopsis of a year of teaching and reflect on the relevance of similar and dissimilar instances in the practitioner's own field setting. Classroom management is again the topic in Task 32. Through autobiographical sketches, practitioners will evaluate personal beliefs and the role of those beliefs in determining classroom management strategies.

## *Task 31*    **Chew and Chat**

*Topic:*    Narrative reflection: Study circles

*Objective:*    The practitioners will discuss episodes from *Among School Children*, by Kidder (1989), and reflect on ethical judgments made by Mrs. Zajac, the book's focus teacher. Occasional questioning on the part of the facilitator may be necessary to prompt discussion.

*Materials:*    *Among School Children*, by Kidder (1989)

*Time:*    1-month preparation; 50-minute discussion

*Procedure:*    1. Ask practitioners to read Kidder's book *Among School Children*. Initiate a "chew and chat" session, where practitioners may bring a meal to eat as they leisurely discuss the story of Mrs. Zajac and the ethical, moral, and sociopolitical ramifications of the daily issues she deals with in her fifth-grade classroom. Kidder provides multiple episodes from his year-long observation of Mrs. Zajac and her students.

   2. Allow practitioners time to express their views on instances in the book. A free discussion of the book, initiated and supported by the practitioners, will bring up points of interest as well as problems to ponder.

*Evaluation:*    Practitioners discussed the problems faced in the book and their relationships to those faced in real-life classroom situations.

*Debriefing:*    1. Were Mrs. Zajac's concerns over favoritism justifiable? If so, in what ways?

   2. What evidence is there that Mrs. Zajac was reflective?

   3. How do problems in Mrs. Zajac's classroom resemble those in yours? How are they different?

   4. What does this book imply about the role of community in education?

   5. Describe attributes of Mrs. Zajac that make her an effective teacher, or an ineffective teacher. Relate instances that support your feelings.

## *Task 32*  Using Autobiographical Sketches to Evaluate Beliefs Regarding Classroom Management Styles

*Topic:* Narrative reflection: Autobiographical sketches

*Objective:* The practitioner will determine the role of past experiences and beliefs in determining his or her current classroom management styles.

*Materials:* A copy of Definition of Classroom Management (Table 3.4); individual copies of Synopsis of Classroom Management Styles (Table 3.5) and Classroom Management Approaches (Table 3.6); clear transparencies

*Time:* 50 minutes

*Procedure:* 1. Discuss with the whole group the definition of classroom management using the Definition of Classroom Management transparency. Allow 10 minutes for practitioners to individually write an autobiographical sketch on two or three remembered incidents from their school days dealing with classroom management. Explain that the experiences would be more beneficial to later reflection if they were from episodes at various time periods throughout formal schooling.

2. When practitioners have finished, ask for factors that have helped to determine their management styles. List factors as presented on a clear transparency. Encourage practitioners to support these factors by relating personal experiences.

3. Group participants into teams of three by having them count off. Use the Classroom Management Approaches document to briefly review various styles of classroom management. Distribute Synopsis of Classroom Management Styles to practitioners. Within each team, practitioners will review classroom environmental controls from the synopsis and determine whether they consider their personal styles to support low, moderate, or high teacher-control environments. Team members should refer to the sketches written during the free-writing experience and discuss how each team member's current classroom environment correlates to incidents recorded in the sketches. Allow 30 minutes.

4. Bring the whole group together to discuss management styles, examples considered by each team, and correlations among experiences and current classroom management styles.

*Evaluation:* Through the use of autobiographical sketches, practitioners investigated the role of personal experiences in determining current classroom management styles.

*Debriefing:* 1. Identify the predominant teacher-control level on your team. Explain possible reasons for this.

2. In which control level do you feel most comfortable? What part did past experience play in reaching this comfort level?

3. What evidence was there that the level of control changed with the context of a situation? What are possible advantages and disadvantages of this change?

4. In retrospect, what other incidents have helped determine management styles?

5. What other areas of teaching might benefit from practitioner reflection using autobiographical sketches?

## REFLECTIVE QUESTIONS

1. Of the three narrative strategies, which do you feel most enhances your reflective thinking ability?

2. How could the chew-and-chat idea be adapted to fit the needs of students in your field setting?

3. Did the autobiographical sketches cause you to remember instances from your past that you had not thought about for quite some time? If so, elaborate.

## ACTION ASSIGNMENTS

### Technical

1. Determine the elements to use in a case study first by observation alone, then by developing a concept map of relevant story elements. Compare and contrast the two techniques.

2. Using *Aunt Skilly and the Stranger*, by Stevens (1994), as a catalyst, engage in a discussion about first impressions with other practitioners. Through observation and case study construction, evaluate the worth of first impressions of students in a field setting.

### Contextual

1. Use Kozol's (1991) *Savage Inequalities* to reflect on alternative practices for diverse learners.

2. Use the elements of narrative to develop a personal philosophy statement on educative practice.

### Dialectical

1. Tell a story to a peer about an incident involving an ethical decision made recently in a field setting. In pairs, analyze the stories to investigate underlying values and assumptions.

2. Write an autobiographical sketch of experiences remembered throughout formal schooling. In pairs, share autobiographical sketches. The readers interpret the sketches of the writers. Discussion should follow to determine how the reader's interpretation fits with that of the writer and the writer's philosophy.

## SUGGESTION FOR SUCCESS

Ensure that sharing occurs in a risk-free environment.

## JOURNALING REFLECTIVE GROWTH

1. How did you feel about sharing life experiences? What helps to raise comfort levels?

2. How can narrative reflection be used with students in a field setting?

3. Did narrative inquiry bring about changes in personal philosophy? Classroom actions?

# 7

# Creating
# Mental Models

*But the greatest thing by far is to be a master of the metaphor. It is the only thing that cannot be learned from others; and it is also a sign of genius because a good metaphor implies an intuitive perception of the similarity in the dissimilar.*

—Aristotle (trans. 1995)

---

### *Chapter Objectives*

**The facilitator will**

- Assist practitioners in demonstrating proficiency in the use of the mental models
- Be able to assess growth in reflective thinking upon application of the strategy
- Analyze personal competence with the strategy to assist practitioners in preparing an action plan that will foster personal reflection upon return to the classroom situation
- Facilitate maintenance of reflective journals to be used by practitioners for personal growth assessment and for peer assessment

---

The analysis of mental models can promote reflective thinking in practitioners. Critics of teacher education programs (Elbaz, 1983; Kagan, 1992; Tabachnick & Zeichner, 1984) contend that unless mental models derived from a practitioner's past experiences are analyzed, education processes and teaching will remain virtually unchanged. Elbaz offered that images in a practitioner's existing schema often invite conformity. Prior experiences in teaching and learning serve as a filter through which the practitioner responds to new ideas. Content and experiences that confirm existing schemata and images of self as teacher are accepted, whereas those that do not are rejected. Unless such images from past experiences are explicitly discussed, it is difficult to bring a practitioner's schema in line with current educative priorities. Two strategies for bringing practitioners' existing constructs to bear are the use of metaphors and the use of repertory grids.

## THE PROCESS OF USING METAPHORS FOR REFLECTIVE THINKING

The use of metaphors by facilitators of practitioners has increased in recent years. A metaphor is the transfer of meaning from one object to another based on a perceived similarity. Pugh, Hicks, Davis, and Venstra (1992) state,

> Metaphorical thinking . . . entails attending to likenesses, to relationships, and to structural features in seeking what Aristotle called "similarities in dissimilarities." It involves identifying conceptual categories that may not be obvious or previously acknowledged. Metaphorical thinking cuts across subject and discipline boundaries by making knowledge in one domain a guide for comprehending knowledge in another, with some transfer of meaning taking place in both directions. Comparison is at the heart of it. . . . To be a metaphorical thinker is to be a constructive learner, one who actively builds bridges from the known to the new. (pp. 4–5)

Metaphors in education stem from the schemata of practitioners. The value of metaphor use is in the relationships practitioners are able to bring into a framing or reframing situation. By analyzing the relationships, schemata can be modified in one of three ways (Rumelhart & Norman, 1981):

| | |
|---|---|
| Accretion | Gradual accumulation of information expanding existing schemata |
| Tuning | The refinement of new information to fit existing schemata |
| Restructuring | The creation of new schemata |

These modifications are closely akin to Piaget's (1975) adaptations of assimilation, accommodation, and equilibrium. As practitioners acquire new insights into educational processes, modifications are attended to. The process is a valid model for restructuring new information for later retrieval.

The benefits of using metaphors in teacher education and staff development are many (Bullough, 1994; Calderhead & Robson, 1991; Grant, 1992; Johnson, 2003; Pugh et al., 1992). Metaphors can

- Aid in self-exploration of beliefs and values
- Help form boundaries and conditions for members
- Assist in simplifying and clarifying problems
- Help to summarize thoughts
- Enable and limit meaning
- Help develop alternative ways of looking at a topic (problem reframing)
- Serve as bridges between a schema and new constructs
- Help form judgments about educational issues
- Assist with communication of abstract ideas
- Demonstrate underlying connections
- Gain insights into what is not yet understood

## THE PROCESS OF USING REPERTORY GRIDS

Kelly (1955) developed the repertory grid technique as an element of his seminal work in personal construct psychology. He posited that mental models are created from elements within individuals' views of the world and that thinking and behavior are guided by these models. Elements have relationships with one another, creating constructs. A *construct* is the way "two elements are similar and contrast with a third" (p. 61). *Repertory grids* are representations of elements and the manner in which elements are construed that reflect personal beliefs about teaching and learning and provide focus for subsequent reflection (Jankowitz, 2003; Smith, 2000; Solas, 1992).

The repertory technique has been used in teacher education for more than 20 years. Munby (1982) studied teacher constructs to examine rationale for using certain methodologies. Olson (1988) evaluated science teachers' perspectives on student behavior. Artilles and Trent (1990) investigated preservice teachers' beliefs about effective teachers, whereas Boei, Corporaal, and Van Hunen (1989) explored student teachers' notions of good teaching.

Benefits of using the repertory grid technique (Solas, 1992) include

- Linking theory with practice
- Providing a means for practitioners to analyze teaching and learning
- Increasing critical thinking regarding personal constructs
- Framing or reframing constructs that produce problems

The procedure for using the repertory technique has four steps. First, elements of a particular model are analyzed. Second, two of the elements are chosen based on a perceived difference from a third. The three chosen elements are then used to create a central concept or construct. The construct should apply to all three elements in the model. Third, the ends of the continuum are described using one- or two-word phrases as much as possible. Then, the element at the opposite pole continuing the dichotomy is described. The poles of the dichotomy created should house a fairly equal number of elements. Finally, practitioners analyze each of the three elements of the model relative to the constructs created.

An example follows. Practitioners are to devise a repertory grid for analyzing five practitioners' classroom management styles. The practitioners become the elements, whereas classroom management is the model. Next, two practitioners are chosen based on a similarity relative to the model. Both practitioners use a teacher-centered approach to classroom management; a third practitioner, chosen as a contrast to these, uses a child-centered approach.

| | |
|---|---|
| Practitioners 1 and 2 | Practitioner 3 |
| Teacher-centered | Child-centered |

Devise dichotomous descriptors for each pole. Examples may be (a) teacher-determined lessons versus student-determined lessons, (b) structured versus unstructured, or (c) teacher-constructed rules versus student-constructed rules. Last, practitioners analyze the two classroom management styles based on personal beliefs, values, and judgments.

## REFLECTIVE ACTIVITIES

### Technical

Practitioners functioning at a technical level will be given the opportunity to explore teacher roles using metaphors, and instructional practices using repertory grids. The practitioners will access past experiences by using both mental models.

## Task 33    Using Metaphors to Explore Teacher Roles

*Topic:*   Mental models: Metaphors

*Objective:*   The practitioner will, after completing Task 28, prepare a two- or three-dimensional metaphorical model of a teacher role.

*Materials:*   Overhead transparency of teacher roles created in Task 28; Definition of a Metaphor (Table 7.1); Benefits of Using Metaphors (Table 7.2)

*Time:*   One 10-minute period; one 50-minute period

*Procedure:*   *Day 1*

Following completion of Task 28, use the overhead transparency developed to support the creation of a metaphorical model of a teacher role by each practitioner. As a whole group, discuss with practitioners the terms *metaphor* and *benefits*. Practitioners select a metaphor of one teacher role that is particularly meaningful to them based on past and current experiences. Using the metaphor, each practitioner will create a model of the teacher role chosen. The models may be completed in two or three dimensions using any medium desired. Models will be explained on Day 2.

*Day 2*

1.  Group practitioners in arbitrary teams of three or four. Practitioners in each team will explain their model to team members, sharing the experiences the model was based on and the relevance of the model to their current field settings. Members should also discuss the various models to determine which model reflects the perspective of all group members. The creator of the model chosen will report to the whole group regarding why the model was chosen as representative of the team. Allow 20 minutes.

2.  In whole-group discussion, models will be shared by the team members who created them. Discuss value of metaphors.

*Evaluation:*   The practitioner created a model that represents a personal metaphor for teacher roles and shared it with team members.

*Debriefing:*   1.  Explain how your model illustrates your perspective of a teacher role.

2.  After viewing other models and listening to explanations by practitioners, explain why you accepted or rejected other models.

3.  What additional metaphors for teacher roles could be added to the beginning list?

4.  In what other areas of education might metaphorical analysis be of value?

5.  What are some alternative models for your personal metaphor of teacher roles?

**Table 7.1**    Definition of a Metaphor

# A transfer of meaning from one object to another on the basis of a perceived similarity.

Copyright © 2005 by Corwin Press. All rights reserved. Reprinted from *Promoting Reflective Thinking in Teachers: 50 Action Strategies*, by Germaine L. Taggart and Alfred P. Wilson. Thousand Oaks, CA: Corwin Press, www.corwinpress.com. Reproduction authorized only for the local school site or nonprofit organization that has purchased this book.

**Table 7.2**     Benefits of Using Metaphors

*Using metaphors can*

- Aid in self-exploration of beliefs and values

- Help form boundaries and conditions of members

- Assist in simplifying and clarifying problems

- Help to summarize thoughts

- Enable understanding of and limit meaning

- Help develop alternative ways of looking at a topic (problem reframing)

- Serve as bridges between schemata and new constructs

- Help form judgments about educational issues

- Assist with communication of abstract ideas

- Demonstrate underlying connections

- Gain insights into what is not yet understood

SOURCE: Adapted from Bullough, (1994); Calderhead and Robson (1991); Grant, (1992); Pugh, Hicks, Davis, and Venstra (1992).

## Task 34  Using Repertory Grids to Explore Instructional Practices

*Topic:*  Mental models: Repertory grid

*Objective:*  The practitioner will construct a repertory grid based on a model of personal constructs dealing with instructional practices.

*Materials:*  Transparencies of Definition of a Repertory Grid (Table 7.3) and Procedure for Creating Repertory Grids (Table 7.4); clear transparencies

*Time:*  50 minutes

*Procedure:*  1.  In a whole-group situation, explain to practitioners the term *repertory grid.* Practitioners will be given 10 minutes of freewriting time to recall instructional practices from their formal schooling, mentioning at least three instances with at least three former teachers.

2.  Ask practitioners to relate experiences to the whole group. Write descriptors of experiences on a clear transparency.

3.  Explain to practitioners that they will be using remembrances of instructional practices to construct a repertory grid. Review procedures for constructing a repertory grid and model the following: Use the instructional process as the model, with former teachers as the model's elements. Use a clear transparency to illustrate the grid as the process continues. Next, choose two former teachers based on their similarity to the model. Choose a third former teacher based on his or her dissimilarity to the model. For instance, both teachers use teacher-centered processes during instruction, whereas a third teacher uses a child-centered approach.

| Former teachers 1 and 2 | Former teacher 3 |
|---|---|
| Teacher-centered | Child-centered |

4.  Devise dichotomous descriptors for each pole. Examples may be (a) teacher-determined lessons versus student-determined lessons, (b) structured versus unstructured, (c) doesn't allow questions versus allows questions, or (d) lectures versus uses discovery learning. In the last step, practitioners will analyze the two styles of instructional process based on personal beliefs, values, and judgments. Instruct practitioners to use the information gleaned from their freewriting to create a repertory grid for the instructional process. Monitor the construction of grids. Look for two or three practitioners willing to transpose their personal grids onto a clear transparency and share them with the whole group.

5.  In a whole-group situation, ask targeted practitioners to share repertory grids with the group. Discuss the makeup of the grid, past experiences that led to their personal constructs, and relevance to their future in teaching.

*Evaluation:* The practitioner created a repertory grid illustrating past experiences with various instructional processes.

*Debriefing:*  1. How did the grid illustrate your past experiences with instructional processes?

2. On what did you base your personal constructs?

3. How are your constructs relevant to your role as practitioner?

4. How are your constructs relevant to your role as learner?

5. What benefit do you see to the use of repertory grids?

**Table 7.3**     Definition of a Repertory Grid

# A representation of elements and the manner in which elements are construed that reflects personal beliefs of teaching and learning and provides focus for subsequent reflection on teaching and learning.

SOURCE: Adapted from Kelly (1955). Used with permission.

**Table 7.4**      Procedure for Creating Repertory Grids

1.  **Analyze** elements of a particular model.

2.  **Develop** construct: two elements chosen based on perceived difference from a third.

3.  **Describe** the dichotomous ends of the continuum.

4.  **Analyze** each of the three elements of the model relative to the constructs created.

SOURCE: Adapted from Kelly (1955). Used with permission.

### Contextual

The practitioner functioning in the contextual mode selects alternatives based on contextual needs and knowledge and value commitments. Analysis, clarification, and validation of principles are used to validate the choice of the alternatives. The following two tasks will (a) assist practitioners in analyzing classroom management styles through development of metaphorical images and (b) explore traits of effective teachers by using the repertory techniques.

## Task 35     Using Metaphors to Explore Classroom Management Styles

*Topic:* Mental models: Metaphors

*Objective:* The practitioner will prepare a two- or three-dimensional model illustrating a metaphor of his or her current preferred management style.

*Materials:* Transparencies of Definition of a Metaphor (Table 7.1) and Benefits of Using Metaphors (Table 7.2); clear transparencies

*Time:* One 15-minute period; one 50-minute period

*Procedure:* *Day 1*

In whole-group situation, discuss with practitioners the term *metaphor* and the benefits of the use of metaphors. Brainstorm possible metaphors for classroom management styles, writing them on a clear transparency as presented. After building a list, practitioners are to select a metaphor for a classroom management style that is particularly meaningful to them based on past and current experiences. Using the metaphor, each practitioner will create a model of the classroom management style chosen. The models may be completed in two or three dimensions using any medium desired. Models will be explained on Day 2.

*Day 2*

1. Group practitioners in arbitrary teams of three or four. Practitioners in each team will explain their model to team members, sharing experiences the model was based on and relevance of the model to their current field setting. Members should also discuss various models to determine one that reflects the perspective of all group members. The creator of the model chosen will report to the whole group, explaining why the model was chosen as representative of the team. Allow 20 minutes.

2. In whole-group discussion, models are shared by the team member who created them. Discuss the value of metaphors.

*Evaluation:* The practitioner created a model that represents a personal metaphor for a preferred classroom management style and shared it with team members.

*Debriefing:* 1. Explain how your newly created model illustrates your perspective on classroom management.

2. After viewing other models and listening to explanations by practitioners, explain why you might accept or reject other models presented.

3. What additional classroom management metaphors could be added to the initial list?

4. In what other areas of education might metaphorical analysis be of value?

5. What are some alternative models that could be used to illustrate your personal metaphor of classroom management?

## *Task 36*  **Using Repertory Grids to Explore Practitioner Traits**

*Topic:* Mental models: Repertory grid

*Objective:* The practitioner will construct a repertory grid based on personal constructs dealing with practitioner traits obtained from interviewing a teacher, student, and community individual.

*Materials:* Transparency of Steps in Interviewing (Table 7.5) and Definition of a Repertory Grid (Table 7.3); a transparency and individual copies of Practitioner Traits (Table 7.6); clear transparencies

*Time:* Two 50-minute periods; one 15-minute interview period

*Procedure:* Day 1

1. Group practitioners into threes based on hair color. Have practitioners initially line up according to hair color, from lightest to darkest. Then, section off by threes.

2. Explain to practitioners that they will be interviewing individuals to determine personal philosophies regarding practitioner traits. An *interview* is a purposeful conversation that is directed by one person to get information from the other. Using the transparency for Table 7.5, discuss Steps in Interviewing:

   A. Prepare four to six open-ended questions on a central issue.

   B. Arrange a time with the subject, informing him or her of the purpose, length of time required, how results will be used, and so forth.

   C. Begin with small talk to develop accord with the subject.

   D. Briefly inform subject of the purpose and that what is said will be treated confidentially.

   E. Ask the predetermined questions. Allow subjects time to talk freely.

   F. Interviewer may use probes such as "Could you explain that?" or ask for specific examples for the purpose of clarification.

   G. Record answers as thoroughly as possible.

   H. Interviewer should not be evaluative.

   I. When the interview is completed, thank the subject for his or her time. As soon after the interview as possible, review the findings and record them in a fashion that will facilitate understanding of the answers at a later date.

   Practitioners will spend the remainder of the time period devising interview questions and determining interviewing strategy.

3. Instruct teams to complete interviews prior to Day 2. One group member interviews a teacher, one interviews a student, and one interviews a community member.

*Day 2*

1.  Discuss the definition of the repertory grid. Distribute copies of Table 7.6 (Practitioner Traits) to practitioners. Each team will create a repertory grid to organize data, feelings, and so forth. Allow 20 minutes.

2.  Ask practitioners to relate their experiences to the whole group. Write descriptors of experiences on a transparency of Table 7.6, Practitioner Traits.

3.  Explain to practitioners that the whole group will be using interview details in constructing a repertory grid. Review the procedure for constructing a repertory grid by modeling the following: Using practitioner traits as the model, interviewees become the model's elements. Use a clear transparency to illustrate the grid as the process continues. Next, two interviewees are chosen based on their similarity to the model. A third interviewee is chosen for his or her dissimilarity to the model. For instance, two interviewees remembered a teacher trait of aloofness, whereas a third interviewee remembered a teacher trait of playing with students on the playground.

| Interviewees 1 and 2 | Interviewee 3 |
|---|---|
| Aloofness | Shared experiences |

Devise dichotomous descriptors for each pole. Examples may be (a) a teacher talking with another teacher on the playground versus a teacher playing with students, (b) a teacher sitting at desk versus a teacher moving about the room, or (c) a lesson involving copying from a book versus the use of manipulatives. Last, practitioners analyze the two practitioner traits based on personal beliefs, values, and judgments.

4.  Discuss makeup of the grid, past experiences that led to personal constructs, and relevance to the practitioners' future in teaching.

*Evaluation:* The practitioner created a repertory grid illustrating interviewee responses to questions regarding practitioner traits.

*Debriefing:*
1.  What were some similarities in responses among interviewees? Differences in responses?

2.  Describe any unexpected responses.

3.  How do responses fall in line with your personal feelings?

4.  On what did interviewees base their personal constructs?

5.  How are personal constructs relevant to one's role as practitioner, based on individuals' perceptions of practitioner traits?

6.  What benefits do you see to the use of repertory grids?

**Table 7.5**    Steps in Interviewing

A. Prepare four to six open-ended questions on a central issue.

B. Arrange a time with the subject, informing the person of purpose, length of time required, how results will be used, and so on.

C. Begin with small talk to develop accord with subject.

D. Briefly inform subject of the purpose and that what is said will be treated confidentially.

E. Ask the predetermined questions. Allow subject time to talk freely.

F. Use probes, if necessary, such as, "Could you explain that?" or ask for specific examples for the purpose of clarification.

G. Record answers as thoroughly as possible.

H. Do not be evaluative or judgmental.

I. When interview is completed, thank the subject for his or her time.

As soon after the interview as possible, review the findings and record them in a fashion that will facilitate understanding of the answers at a later date.

Copyright © 2005 by Corwin Press. All rights reserved. Reprinted from *Promoting Reflective Thinking in Teachers: 50 Action Strategies*, by Germaine L. Taggart and Alfred P. Wilson. Thousand Oaks, CA: Corwin Press, www.corwinpress.com. Reproduction authorized only for the local school site or nonprofit organization that has purchased this book.

**Table 7.6**    Practitioner Traits

|  | Teacher | Student | Community member |
|---|---|---|---|
| Likenesses in responses |  |  |  |
| Differences in responses |  |  |  |
| Unexpected responses |  |  |  |
| Responses that fall in line with personal feelings |  |  |  |

Copyright © 2005 by Corwin Press. All rights reserved. Reprinted from *Promoting Reflective Thinking in Teachers: 50 Action Strategies*, by Germaine L. Taggart and Alfred P. Wilson. Thousand Oaks, CA: Corwin Press, www.corwinpress.com. Reproduction authorized only for the local school site or nonprofit organization that has purchased this book.

## Dialectical

Practitioners reflecting at a dialectical level address problems with self-confidence and incorporate moral, ethical, and sociopolitical issues into decision making. School climate is of major importance to practitioners in terms of moral, ethical, and sociopolitical issues. The dialectical practitioner is given opportunities in Tasks 37 and 38 to assess school climate metaphorically and by using a repertory grid.

## Task 37    Using Metaphors to Explore
Perceptions of School Climate

*Topic:*   Mental models: Metaphors

*Objective:*   The practitioner will prepare a two- or three-dimensional model that illustrates a metaphor of a current perception of school climate.

*Materials:*   Transparencies of Definition of a Metaphor (Table 7.1) and Benefits of Using Metaphors (Table 7.2); clear transparencies

*Time:*   One 15-minute period; one 50-minute period

*Procedure:*   *Day 1*

Explain to the whole group of practitioners the term *metaphor* and the benefits of using metaphors. Brainstorm possible metaphors for the school climate of practitioners' current field settings, writing them on a clear transparency as presented. After building a list, practitioners select a metaphor for school climate that is particularly meaningful to them, based on past and current experiences. Each practitioner will create a metaphorical model of the school climate chosen. The models may be completed in two or three dimensions using any medium desired. Models will be explained on Day 2.

*Day 2*

1. Group practitioners in arbitrary teams of three or four. Practitioners in each team will explain their model to team members, sharing the experiences the model was based on and the relevance of the model to their current field setting. Members should also discuss the various models to determine one that reflects the perspective of all group members. The creator of the model chosen will report to the whole group regarding why the model was chosen as representative of the team. Allow 20 minutes.

2. In a whole-group discussion, models will be shared by the team member who created them. Discuss value of metaphors.

*Evaluation:*   The practitioner created a model that represents a personal metaphor for school climate and shared it with team members.

*Debriefing:*   1. Explain how your newly created model illustrates your perspective on school climate.

2. After viewing other models and listening to explanations by practitioners, explain why your team accepted or rejected other models.

3. What additional school climate metaphors could be added to the initial list?

4. In what other areas of education might metaphorical analysis be of value?

5. What are some alternative models for your personal metaphor of school climate?

*Task 38*  **Using Repertory Grids to
Explore Classroom Climate**

*Topic:* Mental models: Repertory grid

*Objective:* The practitioner will construct a repertory grid based on personal constructs dealing with classroom climate as a model.

*Materials:* Definition of a Repertory Grid (Table 7.3); Procedure for Creating Repertory Grids (Table 7.4); clear transparencies

*Time:* 50 minutes

*Procedure:* 1. In a whole-group situation, explain to practitioners the term *repertory grid.* Practitioners will be given 15 minutes of freewriting time to recall the classroom climate of their current field setting and climates from their formal schooling, mentioning at least two instances in each setting.

2. Ask practitioners to relate experiences to the whole group. Write descriptors of experiences on a clear transparency, as presented.

3. Explain to practitioners that they will be using information from their freewriting to construct a repertory grid. First, review the procedures for constructing a repertory grid by modeling the following: Using the instructional process as the model, former teachers become the model's elements. Use a clear transparency to illustrate the grid as the process continues. Next, two former teachers are chosen based on their similarity to the model. A third is chosen for his or her dissimilarity to the model. For instance, the two teachers use teacher-centered processes during instruction, whereas a third teacher uses a child-centered approach.

| | |
|---|---|
| Former teachers 1 and 2 | Former teacher 3 |
| Teacher-centered | Child-centered |

Devise dichotomous descriptors for each pole. Examples may be (a) teacher-determined lessons versus student-determined lessons, (b) structured versus unstructured, (c) the teacher doesn't allow questions versus the teacher allows questions, or (d) the teacher lectures versus the teacher uses discovery learning. Last, practitioners analyze the two styles of instructional process based on personal beliefs, values, and judgments.

4. Instruct practitioners to use the information gleaned from their freewriting to create their repertory grids for classroom climate. Monitor the construction of grids. Look for two or three practitioners willing to transpose their personal grids onto a clear transparency and share it with the whole group.

5. In a whole-group discussion, ask targeted practitioners to share repertory grids with the group. Discuss the makeup of the grid, past experiences that led to personal constructs, and relevance to the practitioners' future in teaching.

*Evaluation:* The practitioner created a repertory grid illustrating constructs relative to classroom climate.

*Debriefing:*
1. Explain the difference in ease of writing for the current setting versus previous setting(s).

2. On what did you base your personal constructs?

3. How are your constructs relevant to your role as practitioner?

4. How are your constructs relevant to your role as learner?

5. What benefit do you see of the use of repertory grids?

# REFLECTIVE QUESTIONS

1. When building a construct, why is past exprience of such great importance?

2. Why are certain metaphors about education more predominant than others?

# ACTION ASSIGNMENTS

## Technical

1. Review newspaper articles for metaphors regarding education and effective teaching. Create a word wall of the metaphors.

2. Create a repertory grid of constructs dealing with professionalism of practitioners.

## Contextual

1. Select a metaphor regarding effective teaching. Review experiences in your past to analyze when accommodation of the metaphor occurred.

2. Interview administrators, asking the question, "What characteristics do you look for in a teacher candidate?" Prepare a repertory grid of responses.

## Dialectical

1. Interview community members to research mental constructs of effective teaching. After interviews, create repertory grids to reveal constructs. How do these constructs affect community support of education?

2. Compare and contrast personal constructs based on interviews with board of education members, community members, administrators, and practitioners.

## SUGGESTION FOR SUCCESS

Provide ample time for dialogue to promote understanding of personal constructs.

## JOURNALING REFLECTIVE GROWTH

1. Mental constructs are evident everywhere. What mental models are predominant in your communities? Use newspapers and public forums as sources of information. Why do you think these constructs are predominant?

2. Use construct analysis to examine two instances in teaching where the course of action taken was a direct result of a change in beliefs.

# 8

# Promoting Reflective Thinking Through Action Research

*Research or inquiry is a way of life, and teachers who make good decisions about curriculum are continually involved in the research process.*

—Flake, Kuhs, Donnelly, and Ebert (1995)

---

### Chapter Objectives

**The facilitator will**

- Assist practitioners in demonstrating proficiency in the use of action research
- Be able to assess growth in reflective thinking upon application of the strategy
- Analyze personal competence of the strategy to assist practitioners in preparing an action plan that will foster personal reflection upon return to the classroom
- Facilitate maintenance of reflective journals to be used by practitioners for personal growth assessment and for peer assessment

---

Action research is an inquiry-oriented process of self-monitoring that allows practitioners to develop skills, assess disposition toward teaching and learning, and provide systematic experiences that foster growth in teaching and learning. It is an integral part of working in a school. Through action research, practitioners move from technical rationality (Van Manen, 1977) within the classroom to critical examination of classroom processes. Classroom processes do not fall into easily defined categories. Schön (1987) suggests that in framing a problem, teachers construct personal definitions of the problem derived from their own experiences. The practitioner moves beyond implementation of skill to critically thinking about practices and alternatives to those practices along with supporting rationale. Rather than the unquestioned use of a textbook as a framework for teaching, for example, the focus is on the examination of outcomes and issues of learning, such as student needs, and then finding a source or sources of information that support those outcomes and issues.

The rationale for action research has changed little since Dewey's (1933) progressive notions of inquiry were first initiated. Practitioners carry out action research today (Cochran-Smith & Lytle, 1999; Flake et al., 1995; Goodnough, 2001; Hagerty, Hartman, Quate, & Seger, 1994; Kuit, Reay, & Freeman, 2001; Moore, 1999) because

- Investigations are more natural
- Findings are more credible and valid when related to practice
- Practitioners are valuable sources of knowledge regarding classroom situations
- Contemporary research lacks research in practice by practitioners
- Practitioners' research into their own practices may foster change more readily
- There is a gap between research findings and practice in the classroom
- Action research establishes a reflective, problem-solving mindset in practitioners
- Practitioners experience a chance to explore issues of interest and concern
- An opportunity exists for improved professionalism and efficacy
- Practitioners' empowerment is increased

Benefits of action research for practitioners include increased thoughtfulness toward teaching; increased awareness of roles in teaching; and an increased emphasis on appropriate use of strategies, techniques, and models. In addition, practitioners' awareness of gaps between theory and practice and beliefs and practice is heightened, and a keener awareness of student learning and thinking is fostered.

The process of action research has a number of central characteristics (Flake et al., 1995; Gore & Zeichner, 1991; Hagerty et al., 1994; Jacob, 1995; Kemmis & McTaggart, 1988). Practitioners generally follow a process in designing and implementing action research that involves

- Identification of a problem
- Focusing on a central theme or questions
- Deciding on a purpose and goals
- Selecting techniques for monitoring research
- Principles of procedures that include data gathering and analysis
- Application to and implications for existing practice and further research

The process involved in action research correlates well with the reflective thinking model. The first step is to identify a problem. Identification of a problem should stem from a puzzlement or a gap between what is desired and what currently exists. The central theme and subsequent question to support the research develop from considering alternative ways to frame the problem, resulting in a central focus on which to base research. Purpose and goals are established and supported by techniques for monitoring research. Principles of procedures are also researched and decided upon. These principles remind the practitioner of ethical issues surrounding the research (Gore & Zeichner, 1991). Experimentation at this level involves use of the intervention chosen to resolve the problem. Procedures include gathering data by means such as field notes, interviews, sociograms, student artifacts, audio, or videotapings, and through either participant or nonparticipant observations. A second and vital step in carrying out the procedure of action research is data analysis. The process of data analysis involves making meaning of data gathered during research. It is an ongoing and systematic way of determining the value of the intervention and monitoring the research proceedings. Final stages of the process include application considerations and implications for further action or research that may lead to a reframing of the process.

Reflective thinking activities throughout this book may serve as a foundation for action research. Information gleaned from Task 11, "Observing Effective Questioning," may provide the basis for action research surrounding the issue of equity in questioning. Task 12, "Observing Classroom Management Styles," may open up issues such as the type of feedback appropriate to facilitate learning in a low-control classroom environment. Observations, journaling, case studies, and repertory grids may serve to support and inspire the practitioner to adopt an inquiry approach to teaching. Gore and Zeichner (1991) maintain that action research may begin at the initial stage of teacher preparation and be sustained by the practitioner throughout the teaching career. The idea is to construct action research projects as a natural extension of the teaching experience. "The action research provides a focus and a systematic element to their reflection in order to help the [practitioners] work through or work within the 'problem' they experience" (Gore & Zeichner, p. 126).

## REFLECTIVE ACTIVITIES

### Technical

Practitioners engaging in action research at a technical level seek to analyze and improve instruction. Task 39 provides practitioners with a forum for discussing problems within a field setting worthy of further research. The second activity in the section allows practitioners to research and reflect on a self-improvement goal following a microteaching experience prior to attempts to implement the goal.

### Task 39    Preparing for Action
Research: Selecting a Question

*Topic:* Action research

*Objective:* The practitioner will look at problems within a field setting, and decide on a problem of interest that may serve as a research topic.

*Materials:* One newsprint sheet per team of four, placed on the walls around the room; markers; transparency of Definition of a Problem (Table 8.1)

*Time:* 50 minutes

*Procedure:*  1. Group practitioners into teams of four by having them first get into a line from shortest to tallest without conversation among group members. Then section off the teams of four.

2. Buzz groups will discuss the question, "What are problems observed in my field experience?" and discuss the definition of a problem. Allow 10 minutes at the end of which the recorders (shortest individual in each team) list situations on newsprint sheet.

3. In a whole-group discussion, investigate similarities and differences among the situations listed.

4. Allow practitioners to select one situation that would entice them to do further research, then stand by the sheet of newsprint that lists the situations. Practitioners should now be regrouped by area of interest.

5. Newly formed teams of three to five meet to determine a final and central question to be researched. No single-practitioner teams are allowed.

6. Facilitator may choose to vary the procedures found in Task 40 to use as the next activity toward implementing action research.

*Evaluation:* Practitioners formed a central question for research.

*Debriefing:*  1. What were some of the similarities in those situations deemed problematic by practitioners? Differences?

2. Identify situations that were problematic for numerous practitioners.

3. How might the problems be categorized?

4. Is there comfort in identifying and discussing shared problems?

5. Identify situations listed that are beyond your control as a classroom practitioner. Why is this so?

**Table 8.1**    Definition of a Problem

# A dilemma or puzzlement that requires action for resolution.

Copyright © 2005 by Corwin Press. All rights reserved. Reprinted from *Promoting Reflective Thinking in Teachers: 50 Action Strategies* by Germaine Taggart and Alfred P. Wilson. Thousand Oaks, CA: Corwin Press, www.corwinpress.com. Reproduction authorized only for the local school site or nonprofit organization that has purchased this book.

## Task 40    Research for Self-Improvement

*Topic:*  Action research

*Objective:*  The practitioner will select a goal following a microteaching or reflective teaching experience, research literature pertaining to the selected goal, and establish a plan to reach the goal during a subsequent microteaching experience.

*Materials:*  Transparency and individual copies of Action Research Procedure (Table 8.2) goal set following microteaching or reflective teaching experience;

*Time:*  30 minutes

*Procedure:*  1. Once a goal has been set for subsequent microteachings or reflective teaching experiences, assist the practitioners in developing a plan to research means for reaching the goal. Share copies of the Action Research Procedure with practitioners. The problem, central theme or question, and the purpose and goal of the situation have already been established.

2. Using a transparency of the Action Research Procedure, outline the remaining steps in the action research process.

3. Group practitioners according to similar goals. Keep team size at approximately three to five individuals. Allow no single-practitioner teams. Teams are expected to use the procedure to develop a process for reaching their teaching goals. Possible techniques may be to review literature, develop means for monitoring progress, choose criteria for determining whether or not the goal is met, and set a time line for completion.

*Evaluation:*  Practitioners completed a plan of self-improvement toward meeting a self-imposed teaching goal.

*Debriefing:*  1. After discussing your goal with other practitioners, explain your level of interest.

2. What strategies for reaching the goal were discussed that may not have occurred to you before?

3. What do you perceive to be benefits of the action research process?

4. What do you perceive to be detriments to the action research process?

**Table 8.2**    Action Research Procedure

• Identify a problem

• Focus on a central theme or question

• Decide on purpose and goals

• Select techniques for monitoring research

• Perform procedures such as data gathering and analysis

• Determine application to and implications for existing practice and further research

SOURCE: Flake, Kuhs, Donnelly, and Ebert (1995); Gore and Zeichner (1991); Hagerty, Hartman, Quate, and Seger (1994); Jacob (1995); Kemmis and McTaggart (1988).

## Contextual

At the contextual level, decision making of practitioners is enhanced through action research. Practitioners with grade or building commonalities collaborate to plan a small research project. A format will be provided to the researchers that may be adapted to meet their needs. Practitioners using Task 42 will critically examine criteria necessary for informed textbook analysis. A textbook evaluation guideline will be designed.

## *Task 41*    **Collaborative Action Research**

*Topic:* Action research

*Objective:* Practitioners will work in pairs to research a shared problem.

*Materials:* Transparency of Definition of a Problem (Table 8.1); transparency and individual copies of Action Research Procedure (Table 8.2)

*Time:* One 50-minute period; interim research time; one 30-minute period

*Procedure:* *Day 1*

1. Group practitioners into pairs by common grade levels, school assignments, or research interests.

2. Pairs will discuss the question, "What are problems observed in my field experience?" and discuss the definition of a problem. Allow 10 minutes for discussion; at the end of that time, each pair should decide on one central situation that interests them enough to do further research. The problem will need to be phrased as a question.

3. Distribute copies of the Action Research Procedure. Outline the remaining steps in the action research process.

4. Pairs are expected to use the procedure to develop a process for researching their problem. Possible techniques may be to review literature, develop means for monitoring progress, and develop criteria for determining whether or not the goal is met and establish a time line for completion. Provide practitioners with interim research time to carry out the procedure and analyze results.

*Day 2*

1. In a whole-group discussion, talk about successes and problem areas in doing action research. Provide time for each pair to share research with fellow practitioners. Make the environment as relaxing and risk free as possible. You may want to set chairs in a circle.

*Evaluation:* Practitioners completed a research plan to investigate a common problem.

*Debriefing:* 1. Identify common successes and problems found in action research.

2. Was collaborating on a research project a favorable experience for you? Why or why not?

3. What do you perceive to be benefits of the action research process?

4. What do you perceive to be detriments?

5. How might you use action research to support your teaching practice in the future?

## Task 42    Textbook Analysis

*Topic:* Action research

*Objective:* The practitioner will review a textbook series, discuss textbook selection criteria, and then collaborate to produce a textbook analysis form.

*Materials:* One to three complete textbook series covering the grade and age levels in field settings of practitioners; chart paper; individual copies of Action Research Procedure (Table 8.2); Fry's Readability Graph (Figure 8.1); clear transparencies; Sample Textbook Analysis Form (Form 8.1)—optional

*Time:* Three 50-minute periods

*Procedure:* Day 1

1. Group practitioners into teams of three to five by grade or age level taught. Allow no single-practitioner teams.

2. In the first 50-minute period, ask teams to review textbook series. Have teams discuss the central question, "What characteristics of a textbook are important to a practitioner for effective teaching?" Each team selects a recorder, a reporter, and a materials person. The recorder writes down pertinent information to complete the task. The reporter will report as information is requested. And the materials person is responsible for obtaining and organizing materials. A typist may also be selected for typing up the final product.

Day 2

1. In a whole-group discussion, reporters from teams formed during Day 1 present characteristics discussed in the team meetings. The facilitator writes the characteristics on chart paper. When the list is complete, ask teams what categories can be formed by combining some of the characteristics. Possible categories are teacher edition, readability, construction, and so on. Instruct practitioners in how to use Fry's Readability Graph if it is new to them.

2. Instruct practitioners to devise a textbook analysis format that may be used to evaluate textbooks for their classroom. Using a clear transparency, list special considerations suggested by practitioners that have not already been discussed. It is at the facilitator's discretion whether or not to distribute the Sample Textbook Analysis Form at this time. Allow practitioners the remainder of the time to prepare prototypes. The prototypes should be typed and copied for each team member by Day 3.

*Day 3*

Prototypes will be used during this 50-minute time period. Group practitioners in the original teams from Day 1. Provide them with textbook series to review using the prototype instrument. The recorder should write down observations made by team members during the review process. Allow 40 minutes.

*Evaluation:* Practitioners developed a textbook analysis document that evaluates texts in terms of their use for effective teaching. Use the remaining 10 minutes to debrief the task with the practitioners.

*Debriefing:* 1. Identify the characteristics of textbooks that you did not previously know existed.

2. Explain how you arrived at a procedure for completing the assigned task.

3. How might this task have been completed differently if the facilitator had given teams a sample document prior to creation of the prototype? (optional)

4. What are some of the implications of your research?

5. What other research applications may be linked to this type of activity?

**Figure 8.1** Fry's Readability Graph

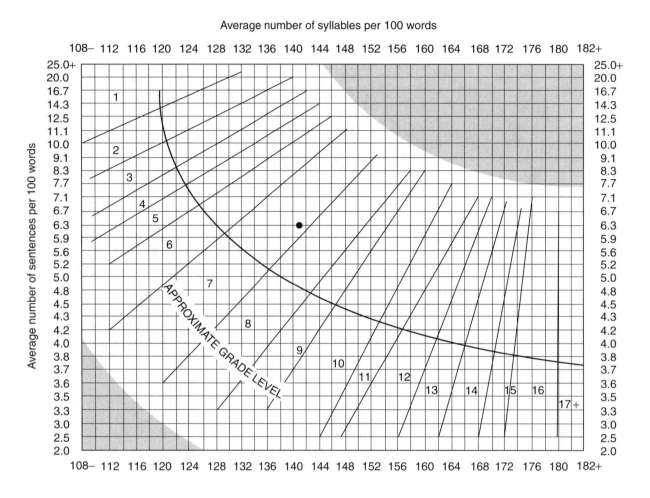

*Expanded Directions for Working Readability Graph*

1. Randomly select three sample passages and count out exactly 100 words each, beginning with the beginning of a sentence. Do count proper nouns, initializations, and numerals.

2. Count the number of sentences in the hundred words, estimating length of the fraction of the last sentence to the nearest one tenth.

3. Count the total number of syllables in the 100-word passage. If you do not have a hand counter available, an easy way is to simply put a mark above every syllable over one in each word; then when you get to the end of the passage, count the number of marks and add 100.

4. Enter graph with average sentence length and average number of syllables; plot dot where the two lines intersect. Area where dot is plotted will give you the approximate grade level.

5. If a great deal of variability is found in syllable count or sentence count, putting more samples into the average is desirable.

Fry, E., *Elementary Reading Instruction,* Figure 8.1. (1977) Reprinted with permission of the McGraw-Hill Companies.

**Form 8.1**     Sample Textbook Analysis Form

## General Information

A. Title of textbook _____

B. Author(s) _____

C. Publisher _____

D. Date of copyright _____

E. Cost _____

F. Publisher or author's suggested readability level _____

G. Readability level _____

## Directions for Completing This Form

A. Rate each question using the scale below.

B. Give each section its own average score determined by aspects you feel are relevant. Comment on these aspects at the end of the evaluation.

C. Record the average scores from each section on the chart below.

D. Find the mean of the Section Averages to determine overall rating of the text.

    I. _____ Physical features     V. _____ Content

   II. _____ Readability          VI. _____ Book parts

  III. _____ Graphics           VII. _____ Skills and activities

  IV. _____ Authorship        VIII. _____ Manual

              Total score   _____

            Total average  _____

Copyright © 2005 by Corwin Press. All rights reserved. Reprinted from *Promoting Reflective Thinking in Teachers: 50 Action Strategies*, by Germaine Taggart. Thousand Oaks, CA: Corwin Press, www.corwinpress.com. Reproduction authorized only for the local school site or nonprofit organization that has purchased this book.

*(Continued)*

**Form 8.1** (Continued)

## Rate the following questions according to the following scale by circling your response:

3 = Good
2 = Average
1 = Poor
NA = Not Applicable

I. Physical features (Section average _____)
   A. 3 2 1 NA   Appealing size and appearance
   B. 3 2 1 NA   Durability

II. Readability (Section average _____)
   A. 3 2 1 NA   Reading level versus grade level
   B. 3 2 1 NA   Presentation of material
   C. 3 2 1 NA   Vocabulary growth (use of new vocabulary)

III. Graphics (Section average _____)
   A. 3 2 1 NA   Well-chosen
   B. 3 2 1 NA   Explanation close to graphic
   C. 3 2 1 NA   Current
   D. 3 2 1 NA   Aesthetic value
   E. 3 2 1 NA   Maps

IV. Authorship (Section average _____)
   A. 3 2 1 NA   Expertise
   B. 3 2 1 NA   Experience in classroom
   C. 3 2 1 NA   Style of writing

V. Content (Section average _____)
   A. 3 2 1 NA   Promotes cognitive growth
   B. 3 2 1 NA   Reflects experiences of today's children
   C. 3 2 1 NA   Free of stereotyping
   D. 3 2 1 NA   Objectives indicated and assessed
   E. 3 2 1 NA   Supports curriculum standards

VI. Book parts (Section average _____)
   A. 3 2 1 NA   Additional suggested reading lists
   B. 3 2 1 NA   Supplementary resource list
   C. 3 2 1 NA   Comprehensive index
   D. 3 2 1 NA   Glossary

Copyright © 2005 by Corwin Press. All rights reserved. Reprinted from *Promoting Reflective Thinking in Teachers: 50 Action Strategies*, by Germaine Taggart. Thousand Oaks, CA: Corwin Press, www.corwinpress.com. Reproduction authorized only for the local school site or nonprofit organization that has purchased this book.

**Form 8.1**

VII. Skills and activities (Section average _____)

    A.  3  2  1  NA   Meets state and district objectives

    B.  3  2  1  NA   Review practices

    C.  3  2  1  NA   Various levels of activities

    D.  3  2  1  NA   Various types of activities

    E.  3  2  1  NA   Assessment fits activities

VIII. Manual (Section average _____)

    A.  3  2  1  NA   Clear, detailed lessons

    B.  3  2  1  NA   Durability

    C.  3  2  1  NA   Practical activities and suggestions

    D.  3  2  1  NA   Enrichment and reteaching activities

## Summary Statements

A. As a teacher, explain your degree of comfort with this material.

B. As a parent, administrator or a member of the community, explain whether or not you would be in favor of this material.

C. Write a composite statement listing strengths and weaknesses of the text.

D. Explain the appropriate use of this text series for diverse populations of students.

E. Provide any additional comments, suggestions, or ideas that you feel are relevant to the adoption of this text.

    *Decision:*   Adopt    _____

                     Reject    _____

                     Evaluator _____

                     Date      _____

Copyright © 2005 by Corwin Press. All rights reserved. Reprinted from *Promoting Reflective Thinking in Teachers: 50 Action Strategies*, by Germaine Taggart. Thousand Oaks, CA: Corwin Press, www.corwinpress.com. Reproduction authorized only for the local school site or nonprofit organization that has purchased this book.

## Dialectical

Practitioners functioning in the dialectical mode are aware of social, political, and ethical issues in school cultures. Action research is carried out to seek change based on ethical, moral, or sociopolitical issues of situations that are problematic to the practitioners. Task 44 provides the practitioners an opportunity to research such issues relative to parental or community involvement.

## *Task 43*   Action Research: Ethical, Moral, or Sociopolitical Issues

*Topic:* Action research

*Objective:* The practitioners will work in pairs to research a shared problem dealing with an ethical, moral, or sociopolitical issue.

*Materials:* Transparency of Definition of a Problem (Table 8.1); transparency and individual copies of Action Research Procedure (Table 8.2)

*Time:* One 50-minute period; interim research time; one 30-minute period

*Procedure:* Day 1

1. Group practitioners into pairs according to common grade levels, school assignments, or research interests.

2. Pairs will discuss the question, "What are some of the problems dealing with moral, ethical, or sociopolitical issues observed in my field experience?" and discuss the definition of a problem. Allow 10 minutes for discussion; at the end of that, each pair should focus on one central situation that interests them enough to do further research. The problem will need to be phrased as a question.

3. Distribute copies of the Action Research Procedure. Outline the remaining steps in the action research process.

4. Pairs are expected to use the procedure to develop a process for researching their problems. Possible techniques may be to review literature, develop means for monitoring progress, set criteria for determining whether or not the goal is met, and establish a time line for completion. Provide practitioners with interim research time to carry out the procedure and analyze results.

Day 2

1. During whole-group discussion, discuss successes and problem areas in doing action research. Provide time for each pair to share research with fellow practitioners. Make the environment as relaxing and risk free as possible. You may want to set chairs in a circle.

*Evaluation:* Practitioners completed a research plan to investigate a common problem.

*Debriefing:* 1. Identify the common successes and problems found in action research.

2. Was collaborating on a research project a favorable experience for you? Why or why not?

3. What do you perceive to be benefits of the action research process?

4. What do you perceive to be detriments?

5. How might you use action research to support your teaching practice in the future?

6. What was your comfort level in dealing with issues relating to your values and beliefs?

**Task 44**    **Action Research: Parent and Community Involvement**

*Topic:* Action research

*Objective:* The practitioners will work in pairs to research a shared problem related to parent and community involvement.

*Materials:* Transparency of Definition of a Problem (Table 8.1); transparency and individual copies of Action Research Procedure (Table 8.2)

*Time:* One 50-minute period; interim research time; one 30-minute period

*Procedure:* *Day 1*

1. Group practitioners into pairs according to common grade levels, school assignments, or research interests.

2. Pairs will discuss the question, "What are problems observed in my field experience that deal with parent or community involvement?" and discuss the definition of a problem. Allow 10 minutes for discussion; at the end of that time, each pair should focus on one central situation that interests them enough to do further research. The problem will need to be phrased as a question.

3. Distribute copies of the Action Research Procedure. Outline the remaining steps in the action research process.

4. Pairs are expected to use the procedure to develop a process for researching their problems. Possible techniques may be to review literature, develop means for monitoring progress, set criteria for determining whether or not the goal is met, and establish a time line for completion. Provide practitioners with interim research time to carry out the procedure and analyze results.

*Day 2*

During whole-group discussion, discuss successes and problem areas in doing action research. Provide time for each pair to share research with fellow practitioners. Make the environment as relaxing and risk free as possible. You may want to set chairs in a circle.

*Evaluation:* Practitioners completed a research plan to investigate a common problem.

*Debriefing:*
1. Identify common successes and problems found in action research.

2. Was collaborating on a research project a favorable experience for you? Why or why not?

3. What do you perceive to be benefits of the action research process?

4. What do you perceive to be detriments?

5. How might you use action research to support your teaching practice in the future?

6. What other situations regarding parent or community involvement would interest you in doing additional action research?

## REFLECTIVE QUESTIONS

1. What characteristics of action research would make you want to use the strategy? Not want to use the strategy?

2. How can action research improve student achievement?

## ACTION ASSIGNMENTS

### Technical

1. Review educational journal articles for innovative strategies for classroom instruction. Then analyze an article's contents, reacting to the article and strategy; relate the relevance of the strategy to current and future field settings and, if the strategy is sound, respond to a practitioner's responsibility regarding using the strategy in practice.

2. Adopt the perspective of an educational theorist, presenting a rationale for your actions and philosophy through a narrative format or by role-playing.

### Contextual

1. Review types of research engaged in up to this point in your career. Through buzz groups, analyze how action research within your own field setting will be similar to or different from past experiences in research.

2. Review with a peer existing tests taken by students in an effort to ascertain the validity and relevance of the tests in producing the type of results and information desired of the instrument.

### Dialectical

1. Research, through interview and document discovery, the views of the media on education. Of particular interest may be media analyses of test results, reactions to unethical teachers, or issues regarding funding. Also of interest may be the impact on public opinion of education supported by the viewpoints of the media.

2. Research student attitudes through observation and survey toward issues such as the use of manipulatives, silent sustained reading, or discovery learning in science.

## SUGGESTION FOR SUCCESS

Provide sufficient time to plan, implement, and discuss research.

## JOURNALING REFLECTIVE GROWTH

1. Assuming action research caused you to look at problems in a different light, what made this possible? If it was not possible, what caused this to be so?

2. Reflect on cognitive growth regarding problems researched. Has there also been social or emotional growth? Reflective growth? Explain.

# 9

# Technology as a Tool for Building Learning Communities

*To know someone here or there with whom you can feel there is under-standing, in spite of distances or thoughts expressed, can make of this earth a garden.*

—Goethe

---

### *Chapter Objectives*

**The facilitator will**

- Assist practitioners in using collaborative approaches to learning in order to enhance discourse and reflection
- Assist practitioners in creating an electronic portfolio to showcase their effectiveness as educators
- Assist practitioners in relaying information to extended communities of learners
- Facilitate use of technology to enhance practitioner discourse and reflection
- Assist practitioners with recognizing emerging technologies that may be useful in improving teaching and learning

# BUILDING LEARNING COMMUNITIES

Research confirms the power of the professional community to heighten educators' efficacy and strengthens the overall capacity of a school (Kruse, Louis, & Bryk, 1995; National Staff Development Council, 2001). Effective learning communities cause individuals and group members to question and challenge practices that have proven ineffective with students and routinely investigate new conceptions of teaching and learning. Such communities maintain an open curiosity about their own practices and tolerate informed dissent. Collaborative communities embrace collective obligations for student success and well-being and develop a collective expertise by employing problem solving, constructive criticism, reflection, and debate. Developing skills in reflective thinking and cognitive thinking greatly enhances the educator's abilities to take responsibility for his or her own teaching effectiveness. Increased responsibility leads to the further development of reflective and cognitive thinking skills, awareness, and control.

Collaboration is more likely to yield benefits when it is supported by (a) substantive knowledge that improves the quality of ideas, plans, and solutions; (b) process knowledge that makes a group effective; and (c) interdisciplinary teams that bring fundamental beliefs to the surface and may reveal points of deep disagreement (Hawley, 2002).

Learning depends on a complex set of personal characteristics that includes values, attitudes, aspirations, level of cognition, preferred learning style, self-confidence, and health. The learning experiences, setting, and interactions within the learning environment are also central to success. They should help learners increase control over their learning and develop new and more efficient skills, styles, and strategies as they pursue learning goals.

Group deliberations require an element of trust among practitioners for discussion to thrive. Trust is not built in an environment where practitioners fear each other's views. However, practitioners should not simply accept alternative perspectives without questioning. Deliberating must take place in an environment where everyone feels free to exchange and discuss ideas in a way that validates those ideas. To monitor the environment, group members should ask themselves the following types of questions:

- What past experiences influenced interpretation of the problem?
- Are potential solutions to the problem acknowledged and reasons provided that support consideration of the solutions?
- What are the consequences of possible solutions and how do those consequences affect the situation?

Although collaboration can take place in many unique ways and in many different settings, practitioners generally utilize five approaches: information exchanging, modeling, coaching, supervising, and mentoring (Henderson, 2001). These five approaches (see Table 9.1) can occur separately or in some combination, and they can involve differing levels of professional commitment:

**Table 9.1** Approaches to Collaboration

- Collaborative exchanging occurs when information is shared.

- Collaborative modeling occurs when one professional demonstrates a teaching skill to one or more colleagues.

- Collaborative coaching refers to an ongoing relationship between two professionals in which one is more experienced than the other.

- Collaborative supervising occurs when a more experienced colleague provides evaluative feedback to one or more colleagues.

- Collaborative mentoring describes a long-term relationship between two professionals in which one has more experience than the other.

- Collegial inquiry occurs when everyone feels that professional empowerment has been enhanced and there is a deep respect for each person's unique inquiry needs, style, and developmental journey.

SOURCE: Henderson (2001).

- Collaborative exchanging occurs when information is shared. Classroom practitioners within the context of a learning community might collaborate in this way when they are trying to assimilate new information in an efficient manner.
- Collaborative modeling occurs when a professional demonstrates a teaching skill to one or more colleagues. This occurs in professional development sessions where practitioners attempt to understand new instructional approaches or when a practitioner invites a colleague to observe the demonstration of an innovative strategy in the classroom.
- Collaborative coaching refers to an ongoing relationship between two professionals in which one is more experienced than the other. A practitioner may engage in the process of helping a colleague by observing classroom practice and dialoguing with the other practitioner about improving classroom instruction.
- Collaborative supervising occurs when a more experienced colleague provides evaluative feedback to one or more colleagues. This approach is different from collaborative coaching in that it involves a judgmental relationship.
- Collaborative mentoring describes a long-term relationship between two professionals in which one has more experience than the other. Mentoring is highly personal and supportive. During the entry year of teaching, many school districts provide a mentor practitioner.

Collaborative exchanging, modeling, coaching, supervising, and mentoring may or may not be infused with the spirit of collegial inquiry. Collegial inquiry only occurs when everyone feels that his or her professional empowerment has been enhanced and there is a deep respect for each person's unique inquiry needs, style, and developmental journey (Henderson, 2001).

## TECHNOLOGY

Communicating through the use of information technology has become a major resource for effective teaching and learning. Such technologies function as the tools that support ongoing, research-based, and results-based teaching.

Chickering and Ehrmann (1996) cite several cost-effective and appropriate ways to use computers, video, and telecommunication technologies that support Chickering's seven principles of good practice (see Table 9.2). The first principle is that good practice encourages student-faculty contacts as the most important factor in student motivation, involvement, and intellectual commitment. Communication technologies such as electronic mail, computer conferencing, and the World Wide Web increase opportunities to converse and to exchange work more rapidly and thoughtfully than ever before. It is often easier to discuss values and personal concerns in writing than orally, since there are fewer inadvertent or ambiguous nonverbal signals. In addition, practitioners from different cultures and language backgrounds often find it easier to communicate electronically because of flexible time opportunities and communication support in the form of language translations and spelling and grammar checks.

**Table 9.2**    Chickering and Gamsons Principles of Good Practice in
Education

*Good practice*

- Encourages student-practitioner contact


- Encourages cooperation among students


- Encourages active learning


- Provides prompt feedback


- Emphasizes time on task


- Communicates high expectations


- Respects diverse talents and ways of learning

From Chickering, A. W. & Ehrmann, S. C. (1996) Implementing the seven principles:
Technology as a lever, *AAHE BULLETIN* 49(2), 3–6. Used with permission.

Reciprocity and cooperation among practitioners is heightened when utilizing technology's versatile formats. The use of study groups, collaborative learning, group problem solving, and discussion of assignments and beliefs can be strengthened through technology. Active learning techniques can easily be incorporated through technologies that foster learning by doing, time-delayed exchanges, simulations, information gathering, and real-time conversations. Practitioners talk about what they are learning, write reflectively about it, relate it to past experiences, and apply it to their daily lives.

Prompt feedback is vital to learning. Electronic communications provides a resource for assessing existing knowledge and competence, a tool for learning new concepts and skills, and a chance to reflect on what was learned and what still needs to be learned. Practitioners can use technology to offer critical observations of performance. Computers provide a rich storage venue for portfolios that give practitioners easy access to products and performances so that knowledge and skills can be assessed over time.

Learning to use one's time well is critical for educators. New technologies can dramatically improve time on task by making communication more efficient, increasing interactions between practitioners, and improving access to information. Technological resources can deliver different methods of learning through powerful visuals and well-organized print; through direct, vicarious, and virtual experiences; and through tasks requiring analysis, synthesis, and evaluation, with applications to real-life situations. They can encourage self-reflection and self-evaluation. They can drive collaboration and group problem solving. Technologies can support learning in more effective ways and broaden repertoires for learning. They can supply structure for those who need it and leave assignments more open-ended for those who do not. Aided by technologies, practitioners with similar motives and talents can work in cohort study groups without constraints of time and space.

## STUDY GROUPS

A study group is a group of people interested in collegial study and action. In schools, study groups can meet to study and to support one another as they do the following:

- Design curriculum and instruction
- Integrate a school's practices and programs
- Study the latest research on teaching and learning
- Monitor the impact of new practices on students and staff
- Analyze and target a schoolwide need

A number of research studies have been conducted that explore how electronic networks support reflection and knowledge that lead to reform-oriented teaching practices (Barnett, Harwood, Keating, & Saam, 2002; Devlin-Scherer & Daly, 2001; Dutt-Donner & Powers, 2000; Levin & Waugh, 1998).

The following recommendations have been established as important to a study group's success:

1. Begin discussions in a face-to-face mode whenever possible. The study group might possibly view a videotape and determine reflection goals or questions for the week.

2. Establish channels of discussion through an asynchronous chat room or discussion board format using the thoughtful questions as a springboard to discussions.

3. Establish participation goals related to definitions of constructive feedback, amount of feedback, and timelines.

4. Encourage practitioners to bring their own set of videotaped lessons to the discussions.

Questions posed in the online environment need to promote deep exploration of the topic and the development of critical thinking and reflection skills. Responses to the questions are neither right nor wrong. They simply serve to stimulate thinking and additional questioning.

Another important element to online discussions is that practitioners provide constructive and extensive feedback to each other. This may occur as part of an ongoing discussion or relate to a specific plan and videotape previously reviewed. Feedback provided creates a point of connection among practitioners and allows them to look at ideas using constructive, collaborative reflection. Covey (1989) states that developing the ability to "seek first to understand, then be understood" promotes interdependence. "Without interdependence, there can be no collaboration, and ultimately no community" (Palloff & Pratt, 1999, p. 125).

# PORTFOLIO DEVELOPMENT

The use of portfolio assessment as a wide-scale assessment tool reflects understandings of the nature of teaching, learning, and assessment. Portfolio assessment appears promising as a way to acknowledge the serious intellectual work of teaching, to capture the complexities of teaching, and to promote professionalism. Although definitions of portfolio assessment vary, they typically include several common features. Practitioner portfolios are purposeful collections of work that are individualized and self-selected; include interrelated yet diverse documents representing growth and achievement; and demonstrate reflection, self-evaluation, and ongoing inquiry (Reis & Villaume, 2002).

Reis and Villaume (2002) used a case study approach to assess the benefits of portfolio assessments on preservice practitioners and their cooperating practitioners. Practitioners in the study frequently mentioned increased reflection as a benefit of the portfolio. The portfolio also contributed to the development of skills through increased organization and planning efforts. Other studies have indicated that portfolios provide for real-world applications and assessments, and that they contribute to ongoing professional development by fostering the development of reflection, scaffolding practical on-the-job skills, and prompting job interview preparation (Dollase, 1998; Klenowski, 2000; Snyder, Lippincott, & Bower, 1998). Benefits to the use of portfolios are documented in Table 9.3.

# REFLECTIVE ACTIVITIES

## Technical

Often those reflecting at a technical level are preservice or new practitioners working to implement effective lessons and strategies. Activities at the technical level should encourage establishment of a relationship with at least one significant colleague to support continuing development and focus on interpersonal skills. Focus on interpersonal skills for open, honest dialogue about teaching. During the second and third years, encourage practitioners to expand their network of colleagues. Suggest that they consider establishing or joining a professional study group.

**Table 9.3**    Benefits to Electronic Portfolios

*Electronic portfolios*

- Provide concrete examples of learning

- Foster discussion and understanding of what has been done

- Encourage personal reflection on the processes of learning

- Assist practitioners in making reflective practice an interactive process

- Provide a rich picture of work so that change over time may be reviewed

- Emphasize process as well as product

- Use technology as a communication tool

- Provide accessibility to a variety of reviewers

- Make the tasks of organizing and sharing collections of artifacts easier, simplifying the task of revision over time

- Facilitate the sharing of experiences and dialogue

- Use a variety of multisensory dimensions to showcase student work

Adapted with permission from Reis and Villaume (2002) and (Dollase, 1998; Klenowski, 2000; & Snyder et al., 1998).

## Task 45    Video as an Observational Tool

*Topic:*  Reflective teaching: Using a videotaped lesson

*Objective:*  The practitioner will analyze and reflect on videotaped episodes of his or her teaching to develop skills for recognizing levels of student achievement.

*Materials:*  Lesson Plan Format (Table 5.9); Rubric for Assessment of Reflection (Table 9.4)

*Time:*  10 minutes preteaching; 30 minutes teaching; 15 minutes reflection

*Procedure:*  Reflective teaching requires the development of a variety of abilities, attitudes, and knowledge. The best way to gain knowledge about reflective teaching is to observe what is happening with your own teaching episodes. Additional support may be obtained by requesting a mentor or colleague to evaluate the videotaped lesson using the same criteria for evaluation. This type of reflection on practice directly affects classroom instruction and student learning.

Videotaped classrooms can provide practitioners with a common framework for discussion, allow multiple viewings of the same classroom, and support multiple perspectives as all practitioners watch and reflect on the same video. The viewing and reviewing of classroom episodes can offer a powerful opportunity for reflecting on one's practice and articulating one's epistemological and pedagogical beliefs (Barnett et al., 2002; Freidus, 2000).

1. Use the Lesson Plan Format to prepare a lesson that you feel fits the academic needs of the students in your classroom. Videotape your lesson and review it to observe how well the strategies fit the subject and your students' needs. Use the evaluation questions below to assess the effectiveness of your lesson. Write a reflective narrative that evaluates your teaching. If possible, allow a mentor or colleague to evaluate the lesson using the same list of questions. Discuss openly the two sets of evaluations.

2. Replan the lesson, making adjustments as necessary. If possible, reteach it to the same or a different group of students to see how effective the changes were. Re-videotape the lesson.

3. Add to your narrative reflection. Were the changes you made for reteaching effective? How do you know that all students learned the concepts or skills written in your objective?

4. Use the Rubric for Assessment of Reflection to analyze your reflection. Set a goal for the next lesson you will teach.

*Evaluation:*  After viewing the videotaped lesson, the practitioner and mentor wrote a reflective evaluation of the practitioner's first lesson, describing the effects of each teaching strategy used. The following questions will help guide discussion and reflection:

1. What were the strengths of the lesson?

2. What were the weaknesses of the lesson?

3. Were content or skills necessary to teach the lesson evident?

4. Were multiple resources used to support the content or skills taught?

5. Were the learning strengths of students considered while planning and teaching the lesson?

6. Were students required to think critically through active engagement and questioning processes?

7. Were higher-level questions asked in an equitable manner?

8. Was appropriate technology incorporated into the lesson?

9. Was appropriate assessment provided that acknowledged learned content or skills?

10. Was enrichment or reteaching of the content or skills utilized when necessary?

11. Was a low-risk classroom climate provided?

*Debriefing:*

1. What advantages were gleaned from the use of the videotaped lesson to determine teaching effectiveness?

2. How did you predetermine the academic needs of the students?

3. How did you predetermine the strategies that would meet those needs?

4. What are the implications of reflecting on the type of practitioner you want to be?

5. How were your mentor's evaluative comments similar to or different from your comments?

6. How will you revise your teaching to be more effective in the future?

**Table 9.4**   Rubric for Assessment of Reflection

| Conceptual framework | Below expectations/ unacceptable 1 | At expectations 2 | Exceeds expectations 3 | Greatly exceeds expectations 4 |
|---|---|---|---|---|
| **Liberally educated** | Response indicates lack of content knowledge, basic skills, and use of resources | Response indicates consideration of adequacy of content knowledge, basic skills, and use of resources at a technical level for the given situation | Response indicates consideration of adequacy of content knowledge, basic skills, and use of resources at a contextual level considering the suitability for each child or alternative situations | Response indicates thoughtful consideration of adequacy of content knowledge, basic skills, and use of resources at a level that embraces the school culture |
| **Professionalism** | Response indicates lack of professional and ethical behavior and the lack of use of materials from professional sources | Response indicates thoughtful consideration of professional and ethical behavior and use of materials from professional sources at a technical level for the given situation | Response indicates thoughtful consideration of professional and ethical behavior, and use of materials from professional sources at a contextual level considering the suitability for each child or alternative situations | Response indicates thoughtful consideration of professional and ethical behavior and use of materials from professional sources at a level that embraces the school culture |
| **Academic discipline and pedagogy** | Response indicates lack of adequacy to design and implement instruction that engages students and causes them to think critically in a supportive environment | Response indicates consideration of adequacy of designing and implementing instruction that engages students, and causes them to think critically in a supportive environment at a technical level for the given situation | Response indicates consideration of adequacy of designing and implementing instruction that engages students and causes them to think critically in a supportive environment at a contextual level considering the suitability for each child or alternative situations | Response indicates thoughtful consideration of adequacy of designing and implementing instruction that engages students and causes them to think critically in a supportive environment at a level that embraces the school culture |
| **Diversity** | Response indicates lack of adequacy of designing and implementing instruction that uses individual strengths to support the learning of a child | Response indicates thoughtful consideration of adequacy of designing and implementing instruction that uses individual strengths to support the learning of a child at a technical level for the given situation | Response indicates thoughtful consideration of adequacy of designing and implementing instruction that uses individual strengths to support the learning of a child at a contextual level considering the suitability for each child or alternative situations | Response indicates thoughtful consideration of adequacy of designing and implementing instruction that uses individual strengths to support the learning of a child at a level that embraces the school culture |

| Conceptual framework | Below expectations/ unacceptable 1 | At expectations 2 | Exceeds expectations 3 | Greatly exceeds expectations 4 |
|---|---|---|---|---|
| **Technology** | Response indicates lack of adequacy to provide instruction utilizing appropriate resources and technology | Response indicates thoughtful consideration of adequacy to provide instruction utilizing appropriate resources and technology at a technical level for the given situation | Response indicates thoughtful consideration of adequacy to provide instruction utilizing appropriate resources and technology at a contextual level considering the suitability for each child and/or alternative situations | Response indicates thoughtful consideration of adequacy to provide instruction utilizing appropriate resources and technology at a level that embraces the school culture |
| **Assessment** | Response indicates lack of adequacy to use formal and informal assessment that compliments instruction and supports the learning environment | Response indicates thoughtful consideration of adequacy to use formal and informal assessment that compliments instruction and supports the learning environment at a technical level for the given situation | Response indicates thoughtful consideration of adequacy to use formal and informal assessment that compliments instruction and supports the learning environment at a contextual level considering the suitability for each child and/or alternative situations | Response indicates thoughtful consideration of adequacy to use formal and informal assessment that compliments instruction and supports the learning environment at a level that embraces the school culture |
| **Reflection** | Response indicates lack of adequacy to reflect critically and utilize the constructive comments from others | Response indicates thoughtful consideration of adequacy to reflect critically and utilize the constructive comments from others at a contextual level considering the suitability for each child or alternative situations | Response indicates thoughtful consideration of adequacy to reflect critically and utilize the constructive comments from others at a contextual level considering the suitability for each child or alternative situations | Response indicates thoughtful consideration of adequacy to reflect critically and utilize the constructive comments from others at a level that embraces the school culture |

Copyright © 2005 by Corwin Press. All rights reserved. Reprinted from *Promoting Reflective Thinking in Teachers: 50 Action Strategies* by Germaine Taggart and Alfred P. Wilson. Thousand Oaks, CA: Corwin Press, www.corwinpress.com. Reproduction authorized only for the local school site or nonprofit organization that has purchased this book.

## Task 46  Reflecting on the Value of Internet Resources

*Topic:*  Internet resources

*Objective:*  The practitioner will reflect upon resources found using the Internet to determine suitability to curriculum and student needs.

*Materials:*  Internet connection; Effective Teaching Strategies (Table 9.5)

*Time:*  Variable

*Procedure:*  Mezirow (1990) states that perspectives are transformed when learners encounter *disorienting dilemmas*—dilemmas that cause the learner to critically assess distortions in the nature and use of knowledge, belief systems, and relationships and *psychic distortions*—suppositions that cause anxiety and inaction. Palloff and Pratt (1999) speak of a "web of learning" that reflects the interdependence of students, peers, technology, content, and the instructor to bring about transformation of perspectives. Through structured use of learning communities, practitioners achieve an awareness of increased competence and independence. "[P]ersonal growth becomes a companion to intellectual growth as the student assumes greater responsibility for the learning process, competence, authority, self-confidence, and a sense of mastery" (Palloff & Pratt, p. 131). Learning communities promote engagement with materials, other practitioners, and transformation of perspectives.

1. Locate a series of Web sites that offer research-based teaching strategies. Explore the academic value of the materials and strategies for meeting the needs of your students and curriculum goals.

    Possible Web sites containing lesson plans to review include the following:

    http://www.csun.edu/~hcedu013/plans.html

    http://dir.yahoo.com/Education/K_12/Teaching/Lesson_Plans

    http://www.lessonplanspage.com/

    http://www.edhelper.com/

    http://www.eduref.org/Virtual/Lessons/index.shtml

    http://www.teachnet.com/lesson/

2. Complete Effective Teaching Strategies using the information you have found. Visit with a small cohort team to share the results of the search and discuss teaching modes and possible implications.

*Evaluation:*  Practitioners compiled a series of Web sites that describe various effective teaching strategies, based on answers to the following questions:

1. How does this lesson or strategy meet the curriculum needs of my district?

2. How does this lesson or strategy meet the needs of my students?

3.  What adjustments must be made to accommodate curriculum directives and the needs of my students?

4.  From what source(s) are the ideas derived?

5.  How can I enhance or expand upon the strategy?

6.  How will this strategy affect each of my students?

7.  What potential impact does this strategy have on the learning of my students? The culture of the school? The existing curriculum?

*Debriefing:*

1.  Has reflecting on Internet resources made you a better practitioner? If so, how?

2.  How do you anticipate that reflecting on Internet resources will affect your learning in the future?

3.  How do you anticipate reflecting on Internet resources will affect your teaching in the future?

4.  How can you transform what you know about using the Internet to glean information to empower students to pursue knowledge on their own?

**Table 9.5**     Effective Teaching Strategies

| Lesson/Strategy | Source/Ideas | Evaluation |
|---|---|---|
|  |  |  |
|  |  |  |
|  |  |  |
|  |  |  |
|  |  |  |

Copyright © 2005 by Corwin Press. All rights reserved. Reprinted from *Promoting Reflective Thinking in Teachers: 50 Action Strategies*, by Germaine L. Taggart and Alfred P. Wilson. Thousand Oaks, CA: Corwin Press, www.corwinpress.com. Reproduction authorized only for the local school site or nonprofit organization that has purchased this book.

## Contextual

Practitioners who have taught for a few years may have developed an expansive repertoire of instructional practices. They have often elevated their understanding of individual and collective inquiry. Practitioners at this stage should consider welcoming a student practitioner or intern into the teaching setting. The mentoring process will provide an opportunity to reexamine their own experiences and beliefs as they open themselves to the examination of teaching practices by another. The community created through such team teaching experiences will help support the contextual practitioner's teaching through increased resources, pedagogical knowledge, technology use, and collaborative reflection.

| *Task 47* | **Learning Communities to Promote Reflection** |

*Topic:* Study groups and reflective teaching

*Objective:* The practitioner will begin a collection of videotaped teaching episodes to use as a tool for self-questioning and study group reflection on teaching effectiveness.

*Materials:* Rubric for Assessment of Reflection (Table 9.4)

*Time:* Variable

*Procedure:* Bridging theory and practice is a gradual process requiring continuous and systematic focus. Improvement in teaching requires looking back and honestly reflecting on your goals and priorities and the manner in which you have tended to the needs of your students in meeting learning goals. Continuous questioning, analysis, and reflection on the part of the practitioner are necessary to ensure effective teaching.

1. An important element of the learning community, whether it is face to face or in the electronic realm, is the development of shared goals related to the learning process. Set aside a block of time (preferably an hour per week) to organize a study group of colleagues to analyze collections of videotaped lessons and lesson plans for the above criteria. Openly discuss the criteria and goals for future teaching episodes.

2. Select three videotaped lessons that you have taught from preplanned lessons using the Lesson Plan Format (Table 5.9) or another format that you feel adequately identifies learner academic objectives, lesson procedures, and evaluation of learning.

*Evaluation:* Practitioners compiled a collection of videotaped lessons and applied the following analysis:

1. Evaluate the effectiveness of the learning experiences of each lesson for your students.

2. Reflect on your instructional strategies and your interaction with students throughout the lessons.

3. Evaluate the student learning experiences and outcomes from the lessons.

4. Describe how you would improve student learning.

5. Determine teaching and learning goals for yourself and individual students based upon review and analysis of the lessons.

6. Evaluate the use of formal and informal assessment strategies to determine students' abilities to meet desired objectives.

*Debriefing:* 1. How will the videotaped teaching episodes be utilized as you begin to create your personal teaching portfolio?

2. What goals should be outlined for effective structure of the study group?

3. Discuss the reward of the study group process.

4. How will accountability be built into the process?

5. How comfortable do you feel with the study group process?

6. What are the feelings among the group about the collaborative work process?

7. Did the collaborative process contribute to the learning goals of the group, individuals within the group, and those of the students?

## Task 48    Linking Electronic Portfolios to Reflective Writing

*Topic:* Electronic portfolios

*Objective:* The practitioner will use an electronic portfolio as a tool for showcasing reflective entries about professional practice.

*Materials:* Reflective Thinking Model (Figure 1.2); Benefits to Electronic Portfolios (Table 9.3); Basic Steps to Electronic Portfolio Collection (Table 9.6); A Herringbone Graphic Organizer (Table 9.7)

*Time:* 1 hour

*Procedure:* The use of reflective writing with submission to an electronic portfolio embraces the constructivist belief that teaching is an active and learner-centered process. Practitioners should recognize that they can use their own perceptions of ideas and experiences to scaffold learning.

Electronic portfolios emphasize process as well as product. They are multisensory in nature, often including images, sound, video, text, and multimedia products. Technology utilization is emphasized as a tool for learning—a concept that practitioners can help their students to experience. The most successful electronic portfolios link reflective practice with products and performances that support and showcase acquisition of practical skills and knowledge (Shulman, 1998).

Benefits to Electronic Portfolios include the following:

- Providing concrete examples of learning
- Fostering discussion and understanding of what has been done
- Encouraging personal reflection on the processes of learning
- Assisting practitioners in making reflective practice an interactive process
- Providing a rich picture of work so that change over time may be reviewed
- Emphasizing process as well as product
- Using technology as a communication tool
- Accessibility to a variety of reviewers
- Making the tasks of organizing and sharing collections of artifacts easier and easing the task of revision over time
- Facilitating the sharing of experiences and dialogue
- Using a variety of multisensory dimensions to showcase student work

There are many venues for housing electronic portfolios. These include relational databases such as FileMaker Pro 4.0 or Microsoft Access; hypermedia "card" formats such as HyperStudio, HyperCard, Digital Chisel, or SuperLink +; multimedia authoring software such as Macromedia Authorware or Macromedia Director; network-compatible hypermedia such as Web pages or Adobe Acrobat; and office "suite" multimedia slide shows such as Microsoft PowerPoint or AppleWorks. There are also several commercial software packages appropriate for creating electronic portfolios, including Grady Profile and Persona Plus. Whichever venue is chosen, ongoing professional development to assist practitioners with the development of portfolios is absolutely necessary to ensure that technological and logistical problems do not get in the way of the reflection process.

Outline the four basic steps to electronic portfolio collection (see Table 9.6) for the practitioners. Practitioners should collectively engage in small-group discussion of artifact collection, selection, reflection, and projection until a comfort level has been established.

*Collection:* Assemble work samples and other supporting materials that demonstrate the processes and products of the practitioner's learning. Consider the context in which and for which the artifact was produced and the processes involved in producing it as well as the components and function of the artifact. Consider reviewing an artifact using a herringbone organization tool (see Table 9.7). The herringbone is a graphic organizer designed to help students identify separate causes and effects when planning a course of action or when analyzing the cause of a particular consequence, result, or effect. The organizer should contain the following principles: Who were the stakeholders? What was the process? What was the product? What is the context of the artifact (when and where was it produced)? How was it produced?

*Selection:* Selects examples of best work, work that showcases improvement or self-reflection, or work that exemplifies a specific criterion such as a professional standard.

*Reflection:* Reflection should involve thoughtful analysis of each item included in the portfolio to identify ways in which learning was affected. Look for purpose, intended audience, value, and significance, along with the effectiveness of the selected artifact and the experience represented (Bullough & Gitlin, 2001).

*Projection:* Projection involves examining ways to improve; to set goals for the future; or to identify patterns, strengths, and areas of improvement. The practitioner relates what was done to what is known in the profession about effective learning and teaching. Returning to the Reflective Thinking Model in Chapter 1 (Table 1.2) will facilitate outlining this process for practitioners.

- **Problem:** This is about the problem at hand. Is there a student who has difficulty grasping a concept in mathematics? Does the practitioner need additional resources to teach an integrated concept? Is there a problem with group or cooperative learning activities? Is the management plan for the classroom not working to bring about on-task behaviors for all students? Practitioners should provide a brief, yet detailed, analysis of the problem. Step outside the situation, if possible, to derive the deeper roots of the problem. This can be done by videotaping episodes, visiting with mentors or colleagues, or having a colleague or administrator observe the nature of the problem.

- **Framing/reframing:** Analyze the problem through information derived from observations, reflection, moral judgments, schema, and context.

- **Data Gathering:** Information gathered through the process of reflection provides a unique opportunity to learn.

- **Intervention:** Consider possible solution sets for resolving the dilemma.

- **Experimentation:** Investigate the value of the intervention. Use observations, self- and peer judgments, and other available resources.

- **Evaluation:** Evaluate for effectiveness, growth, and the ability of the intervention to bring about desired change. Accept or reject the intervention based upon this evaluation.

*Evaluation:* Evaluation of the electronic portfolio entries is based upon several categories: (a) description of the entry, (b) analysis of why and how the evidence meets a particular standard, (c) appraisal of evidence against effectiveness for teaching and learning, as well as against the goals, values, and teaching practice and how practitioners will do things differently in the future. A reflective matrix is provided in Table 9.8. Possible reflective prompts for evaluating the portfolio are found in Table 9.9.

*Debriefing:* 1. What elements of artifact collection did you find most rewarding? Most difficult?

2. The herringbone organizer can serve as a useful tool for analyzing artifacts. How might you use the cause-and-effect thought map in classroom instruction?

3. Beginning the portfolio process as a member of a team should have provided you with helpful insight. What rules stemming from this collective process might you recommend to others?

4. What, if any, key insights into your teaching did you derive from the portfolio experience?

**Table 9.6**    Basic Steps to Electronic Portfolio Collection

**Collection**

**Selection**

**Reflection**

**Projection**

**Elements of Reflective Thinking Model:**

- **Problem**

- **Framing/reframing**

- **Data gathering**

- **Intervention**

- **Experimentation**

- **Evaluation**

Copyright © 2005 by Corwin Press. All rights reserved. Reprinted from *Promoting Reflective Thinking in Teachers: 50 Action Strategies*, by Germaine L. Taggart and Alfred P. Wilson. Thousand Oaks, CA: Corwin Press, www.corwinpress.com. Reproduction authorized only for the local school site or nonprofit organization that has purchased this book.

**Table 9.7a**    A Herringbone Graphic Organizer

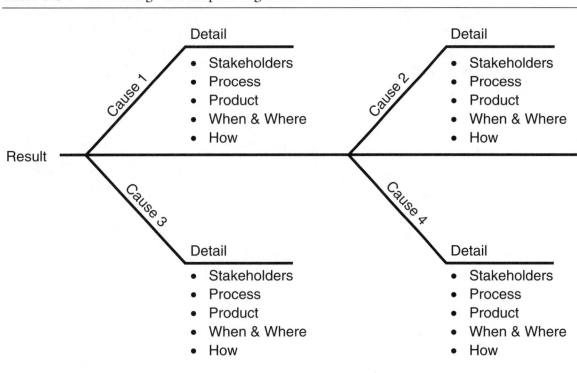

**Table 9.7b**

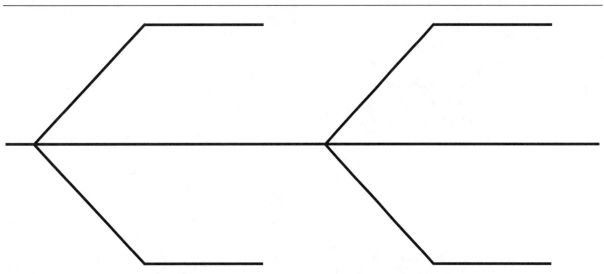

Copyright © 2005 by Corwin Press. All rights reserved. Reprinted from *Promoting Reflective Thinking in Teachers: 50 Action Strategies,* by Germaine L. Taggart and Alfred P. Wilson. Thousand Oaks, CA: Corwin Press, www.corwinpress.com. Reproduction authorized only for the local school site or nonprofit organization that has purchased this book.

**Table 9.8**     Electronic Portfolio Reflections

| Teaching Standard/Goal | Artifact Description | Indicators of Success | Evidence or Comments |
|---|---|---|---|
| **Knowledge of content** | | | |
| **Knowledge and use of pedagogy** | | | |
| **Establishing a culture of learning** | | | |
| **Classroom management** | | | |
| **Provisions for addressing diversity** | | | |
| **Assessment** | | | |

Copyright © 2005 by Corwin Press. All rights reserved. Reprinted from *Promoting Reflective Thinking in Teachers: 50 Action Strategies,* by Germaine L. Taggart and Alfred P. Wilson. Thousand Oaks, CA: Corwin Press, www.corwinpress.com. Reproduction authorized only for the local school site or nonprofit organization that has purchased this book.

**Table 9.9**   Electronic Portfolio Prompts

| | **Sample Question Prompts** |
|---|---|
| **1. Liberally Educated With Knowledge of Subject Area** <br> Demonstrates knowledge of basic skills, subject matter content and pedagogy; utilizes diverse resources from liberal arts and sciences; creates learning experiences meaningful to students | Do I respond accurately and appropriately to student questions regarding content or know where to look for answers? <br> Do I represent and use differing viewpoints, theories, or "ways of knowing"? <br> Do I use authentic material to make lessons relevant? <br> Are students attentive, concentrating, receiving, responding, actively engaging, valuing, comparing, and integrating lesson material? <br> Do I create interdisciplinary learning experiences that allow all students to integrate knowledge, skills, and methods of inquiry from several subject areas? |
| **2. Pedagogical Planning of Supportive Environments** <br> Designs instruction and develops lesson plans that encourage critical thinking and problem solving; engages students in learning; establishes a culture of learning | Do I promote action learning and direct involvement of students? <br> Do I use concrete activities? Interesting and challenging activities? <br> Do I promote learner interaction and reflection <br> Do I provide assistance, scaffolding, or cues? <br> Are students using or developing a template for problem solving? <br> Do I create a learning community in which all students assume responsibility for themselves and one another? <br> Do I allow students time to work collaboratively as well as independently? |
| **3. Management of Instructional Technology** <br> Prepares materials in advance; manages classroom procedures effectively; appropriately uses technological resources | Are my lesson objectives and purpose clearly defined for students? <br> Do I have resources ready to use? <br> Do I apply both formative and summative evaluation techniques? <br> Does my lesson have closure? <br> Do I select appropriate technology to illustrate lesson concepts? <br> Do I utilize a variety of appropriate instructional technology and tools to prepare and deliver instruction? <br> Do I incorporate organizational tools to assist my students' learning? <br> Have I assessed the value of my lessons according to the prescribed curriculum? <br> Do my lesson objectives meet the needs and interests of my students? |
| **4. Management and Student Behavior** <br> Follows and establishes rules and ethical standards; monitors student behavior; stops aberrant behavior; organizes physical space and uses strategies to encourage critical thinking and problem solving; demonstrates understanding of individual and group motivation | Does my classroom provide an atmosphere of safety and comfort? <br> Is there enough space for students to move freely and work without distractions? <br> Does everyone demonstrate respect and cooperation? Value achievement? <br> Do I remind students how and where to find solutions or how to use problem-solving techniques? <br> Do I expect students to be responsible for their actions? <br> Do I encourage responsible behavior in the classroom? |

*(Continued)*

**234** **Table 9.9** (Continued)

## 5. Presentations Address Diverse Needs

Reviews, introduces, summarizes, plans strategies; delivers clear instruction/assignments with relevant examples/demonstrations; maintains appropriate levels of questions, pace, instructional technology, and on-task engagement to address diversity

*Do I demonstrate an awareness of different student backgrounds?*
*Do I use resources from a variety of cultures and perspectives?*
*Do I provide opportunities for students to learn from each other?*
*Do I utilize individual strengths?*
*Do I address multiple learning styles?*
*Do I use software or Web pages to provide meaning for every student?*
*Do I provide opportunities for heterogeneous grouping of students? Encourage students to share mental processes they use for reaching concepts and conclusions?*
*Do I select alternative teaching strategies and materials?*

## 6. Assessment

Uses formal and informal assessment strategies to evaluate student learning; provides feedback to students; maintains accurate records; demonstrates flexibility and responsiveness

*Do I apply cognitive, humanistic, and behaviorist theories to gather information about each student in order to prepare and assess effective instructional activities?*
*Do I use multiple assessments theory to address strengths and weaknesses and provide meaningful learning experiences for each student?*
*Do I use multiple assessments, such as practitioner-made tests, checklists, rating scales, observations, discussion, computer-based, authentic-based, project-based, and standardized tests?*
*Can I design a rubric that expands on the details included in other forms of assessment?*
*Do I convey clear descriptions of performance expectations?*
*Do I design exams that coincide with lesson material?*
*Do I record student needs and progress toward goals?*
*Do I provide a variety of reading material at various levels and interests related to subject or discipline?*
*Do I use teachable moments (showing flexibility to change schedule as needed and appropriate)?*
*Do I welcome spontaneous sharing by students as related to lesson objectives?*

## 7. Reflective Teaching

Uses self-reflection and reflection of others; continues to grow and develop professionally; demonstrates positive rapport; exhibits evidence of effective teaching in an online teaching portfolio

*Do I routinely and purposefully deliberate or reflect on teaching?*
*Do I openly explore classroom decisions and search for alternative explanations for classroom events?*
*Do I take responsibility for actions and classroom events?*
*Do I want to learn both theory and practice?*
*Do I keep a journal about teaching?*
*Do I confront decisions openly by asking questions about the interests, objectives, and standards served?*
*Do I record successful and effective lessons in a teaching portfolio?*
*Do I listen to ideas and criticism and articulate a plan of action for improvement?*
*Do I participate in collegial activities designed to make the entire school a productive learning environment?*

Copyright © 2005 by Corwin Press. All rights reserved. Reprinted from *Promoting Reflective Thinking in Teachers: 50 Action Strategies*, by Germaine L. Taggart and Alfred P. Wilson. Thousand Oaks, CA: Corwin Press. www.corwinpress.com. Reproduction authorized only for the local school site or nonprofit organization that has purchased this book.

## Dialectical

Practitioners who have taught 10 or more years must ask themselves questions that reveal whether or not they are teaching as effectively as possible: Are you the practitioner that you envisioned yourself being? What colleagues have been key factors in your professional development? What is the focus of your inquiry now? Have you continued your formal education in graduate school? Have you intentionally changed your job or school assignments to work in a situation more in line with your beliefs? Are you initiating inquiry within the learning community and participating in collective inquiry with staff, parents, and students? Are you looking for ways to expand your influence past the learning community to the larger community of your profession or your city or town? The following tasks will assist the veteran practitioner in reflecting on his or her role in the educational community.

| *Task 49* | **Online Peer Mentoring** |

*Topic:* Reflective teaching

*Objective:* The practitioner will engage in meaningful online discussions with composite mentoring team members.

*Materials:* Computer with World Wide Web capabilities or email or chat room potential

*Time:* 1 hour

*Procedure:* Reflection and journaling as part of the mentoring process is one strategy to address challenges that many practitioners face. Practitioners use reflection and journaling as a way to communicate thoughts and feelings about teaching and learning and beliefs and behaviors regarding members of the school community, especially their students. Reflection and journaling are effective in uncovering both the frustrations and expectations of practitioners. Principals should consider implementing reflection and journaling as part of a specific set of strategies to assist practitioners with ongoing professional improvement.

One way of assisting practitioners with their reflections is through the use of peer mentors. Often in mentorship programs, each practitioner is assigned just one mentor. However, Packard (2003) suggests composite mentoring as a viable alternative. Composite mentoring involves the strategic selection of a diverse set of mentors who guide practitioners to take a more active role in their own mentoring experiences. Educators considering National Board certification would find composite mentoring very helpful as a means for validating the process of planning, teaching, analyzing, and reflecting that is inherent in the National Board certification process.

Principals should be thoughtful and proactive about the selection of mentors. As Brock (1990) and Valli (1997) have reported, exemplary practitioners do not always make exemplary mentors. Every effort should be made to match practitioners with mentors who are willing to work with them and are committed to success. Principals should also make every effort to pair practitioners with mentors who have experience and expertise in the same subject matter, teach in close proximity, and have the same preparation period.

The facilitator should establish a composite team of veterans to work with new practitioners. Considerations for teaming should include similar experiences or teaching assignments, grade levels, or professional interests. Allow teams time to meet face-to-face so that they may begin creating a network through the following:

- Discussing interests, concerns, goals, and so on
- Developing an atmosphere of respect and trust
- Becoming committed to the team
- Sharing e-mail addresses
- Setting schedules for face-to-face meeting times on a regular basis, preferably no less than once a month
- Discussing preparations necessary before each meeting
- Establishing a common set of definitions, goals, and expectations for constructive critiques

- Establishing parameters and expectations for online discussion and communications, such as length and frequency of discussions
- Considering strategies for maintaining a high degree of communication and assistance

A useful tool for helping to maintain consistency and high expectations is to follow the Collaborative Professional Development Process outlined in Chapter 4 of Bella's (2004) *Reflective Analysis of Student Work: Improving Teaching Through Collaboration*.

*Evaluation:* The facilitator met with the teams and participated in online discussion periodically to assure that the teams followed the criteria established or troubleshot as needed.

*Debriefing:*

1. What elements of the face-to-face team meetings did you find most rewarding? Most difficult?

2. How might you use the collaborative teaming process in your classroom?

3. What have you learned about your practice through the face-to-face and online discussions?

4. What must you address in order to strengthen your practice?

5. Was your evaluation of your classroom and professional practice the same as your colleagues? How were they alike? How were they different?

6. What area(s) should you, as the practitioner, set as a future priority? (You may find it helpful to link this discussion to creation of the professional action plan or action research plans from previous chapters.)

| *Task 50* | **Technology to Support the Learning Community** |

*Topic:* Community support

*Objective:* The practitioner will investigate uses of technology for communication to the learning community about the goals and operations of the school.

*Materials:* Computer with Internet and word processing capabilities

*Time:* 1 hour

*Procedure:* The classroom is a microcosm of society. Children's actions and interactions often parrot those of their parents and friends. Thus a school's culture is greatly influenced by the beliefs and norms of the parents and community members. In order to develop a strong support system for student learning, parents and community members must have an understanding of the school culture and the educational guidelines established through extraneous educational agencies. Timely and appropriate communication is the vehicle for developing such understanding.

Parents want their children to succeed in school, and they want more say in what happens in the classroom. They desire more information about their children's curriculum, and occasionally, they want real decision-making power. Practitioners usually welcome parents who take an interest in their child's education. They know the difference a caring and attentive parent can make in a child's life and academic career. By forming effective partnerships with parents, practitioners can get a boost in helping their students to succeed.

Improved channels of communication foster understanding, caring, and collaboration between the classroom and home. It also is our best hope for increasing support for our educational institutions. Researchers recommend using the following strategies to improve interactions with parents:

1. *Make It Positive*    Research has shown that practitioners communicate with parents most often when the child misbehaves. It is also important to let parents know what their child is doing well. This actually helps parents be more responsive to those areas where their child needs work.

2. *Make It Practical*    Give parents resources to understand the curriculum. Then be specific about where students are having trouble. Make specific suggestions about what parents can do to help their child overcome the difficulties they are having with schoolwork.

3. *Make It Personal*    Although there is not adequate time in your day to write personal messages for every student in your class, collaboration between parents and practitioners is increased when parents read something personal about their own child. Try to include personalized messages to parents whenever possible.

No Child Left Behind (NCLB) sets high expectations for communicating with parents and community members about student achievement. Thus far, the World Wide Web has been used by a limited number of schools to inform parents and students about progress, but this information has been confined mostly to class assignments and schedules. Community engagement gets everyone involved in the community of the school, and technology can and should be used to help facilitate this. E-mailing parents regarding events from the classroom, lesson updates, or personal notes about the successes of their children is a good place to start, as are posting activity calendars and school report cards on the school's Web site. Demographic and test-score data should also be easily accessible to all Web site visitors, so long as student privacy rights are respected.

The volume of paperwork and data collection in education has grown at an exponential rate in the last 10 years, as the demands for accountability have increased. Although technology has helped in data gathering and has provided some relief, the value that such information can offer to the education community must be gleaned by the practitioner.

Schools and districts are also turning to the Internet as a vehicle to highlight successful programs, inform parents who are new to the community, and adhere to state requirements to provide school achievement reports. Internet-based technologies are changing the way educators, parents, and community members exchange information and provide support. As educators become more comfortable communicating via technology, and as communication software becomes more robust, technology will play an increasing role in supporting community connectedness to schools.

Along with these uses for technology in fostering communication among the school community, consider the following strategies:

1. Slide shows or classroom technology projects could be shown on the school's Web site. This is a great way to demonstrate to parents how technology is being used to enhance their child's education.

2. When parents come into the school for conferences, computers could be set up to display students' multimedia projects.

3. Using Hyperstudio, students could write a letter to their parents telling them about their experiences each week at school.

4. Have the students keep electronic portfolios to show growth throughout the year.

5. A virtual tour could be set up for parents and students interested in attending your school and could serve as an orientation. Information such as course offerings and special teams or events could be included on the CD-ROM showcasing your school.

6. Host a Technology Fair. Invite parents or community members who use technology every day on the job to come in and form a panel or set up a display to demonstrate to students how they use technology.

7. Digital images could be taken in classrooms depicting literacy circles, cooperative group work, student presentations, and so on. Images could be printed and shared with parents.

8. Newsletters could be developed using desktop publishing programs, printed, and sent home to keep parents informed.

9. The school's Web site could be used to inform parents of upcoming events, such as book fairs, read-a-thons, picture day, report cards, and so on.

10. Primary practitioners who send home traveling books may consider creating a digital book and posting it on the Internet to be downloaded and shared by students with their parents at home.

11. Create a Web site about your class. List long- and short-term assignments, daily objectives, lesson plans, homework assignments, and any information that you think parents may want to know about school and class activities. For families with access to a computer, this is a valuable means of communication, especially if parents can contact you via a link on the Web site.

Have teams of practitioners select one of the strategies listed or develop one of their own as a means to communicate more effectively with the educational community. Develop a plan of action for carrying out the communication strategy. If time permits, teams may actually begin to work on the task.

*Evaluation:* After the team has developed the strategy for communication, an action research project (see Chapter 8) can be devised and executed to assess the effectiveness of the strategy.

*Debriefing:* 1. With what phases or parts of the project did you feel most comfortable? Why?

2. What phases or parts of the project did you find to be the most challenging? Why?

3. Specifically, how could you change or improve the phase steps and worksheets?

4. What kinds of resources did you find most helpful in working on this project?

5. What kinds of resources were missing but would have been helpful?

6. What do you want to find out more about or learn how to do for future projects? What resources might you access to do that?

7. How can practitioners, parents, students, and community members be involved in the development of school and district technology?

8. What technical standards are necessary to allow communication among classrooms within a school, among schools within a district, or within the educational community?

9. Does your plan describe how parents can best use existing networks and communication systems to facilitate communication with educators regarding student progress, assessment results, and support resources?

# REFLECTIVE QUESTIONS

1. How do I define learning? What do I hope to see as learning outcomes for myself?

2. Do I routinely incorporate collaborative experiences into my classroom?

3. How can the use of technology by practitioners improve student achievement?

4. Can a collaborative environment on the part of practitioners aid in raising student achievement? If so, how?

5. How can you involve the community in district and school strategic technology planning efforts?

# ACTION ASSIGNMENTS

## Technical

1. Interview a district administrator to assess his or her perspective on collaboration among practitioners in the district. What aspects are welcomed? What aspects have proven to be negative?

2. Meet as a team with other practitioners to assess the value of existing classroom resources. Consider classroom manipulatives, online resources, hard copy resources, available field trips and speakers, and so on. Can technology prove more effective for bringing about student learning than these traditional resources?

## Contextual

1. Survey administrators, practitioners, and community members to get a sense of the multiple uses of technology by the district, by the administrators, by classroom teachers, and your community. Analyze the results, then compare and contrast with the district's technology plan.

2. Form a study circle (see page 143) to assess the value of technology when developing and administering formative and summative assessments.

## Dialectical

1. Which teaching strategies are you most likely to employ in your classroom? Why? How do they fit your emerging style of teaching? Have you selected an adequate variety of strategies to motivate students with different learning styles and needs? Which strategies would you avoid using? Why? How can technology enhance these teaching strategies?

2. Generate a metaphor (see page 166) that captures your teaching self as it relates with the educational community. You may identify areas of personal

importance, then apply them to teaching; or metaphorically link items of personal meaning such as unique qualities, heritage, beliefs, or life aspirations to the world of teaching. Add a reflective statement that identifies how you came up with your metaphor. Share your metaphor and reflection with a peer or mentor.

## SUGGESTIONS FOR SUCCESS

1. Provide sufficient time for practitioners to develop a comfort level with the technology.

2. Sufficient time is also needed when effective collaborative teams are being developed and nurtured.

## JOURNALING REFLECTIVE GROWTH

1. Reflect on the ability of technology to reach children and parents in a way that face-to-face interactions cannot. In other words, why should we bother with the technology?

2. Why would composite teams prove more functional than paired teams of practitioners? Is there a time when paired teams would be more beneficial?

3. Reflect on your comfort level with the use of technology to enhance educational communications. With what strategies are you comfortable? Uncomfortable? Develop a plan for easing your discomfort.

# References

Aristotle, E. (1995). *Politics* (E. Barker Trans.). Oxford, NY: Oxford University Press.

Aronson, E., Blaney, N., Stephan, D., Sikes, J., & Snapp, M. (1978). *The jigsaw classroom.* Beverly Hills, CA: Sage.

Artilles, A. J., & Trent, S. C. (1990). *Characteristics and constructs: Prospective teachers' descriptions of effective teachers.* (ERIC Document Reproduction Service No. ED340691).

Bandura, A. (1968). *Social foundations of thought and action: A social cognitive theory.* Englewood Cliffs, NJ: Prentice Hall.

Barnett, M., Harwood, W., Keating, T. & Saam, J. (2002). Using emerging technologies to help bridge the gap between university theory and classroom practice: Challenges and successes. *School Science and Mathematics, 102*(6), 299–313.

Beattie, M. (1995). New prospects for teacher education: Narrative ways of knowing teaching and teacher learning. *Educational Research, 37*(1), 53–70.

Bella, N. J. (2004). *Reflective analysis of student work: Improving teaching through collaboration.* Thousand Oaks, CA: Corwin.

Berne, E. (1964). *Games people play: The basic handbook of transactional analysis.* New York: Random House.

Bigge, M. L., & Shermis, S. S. (1992). *Learning theories for teachers* (5th ed.). New York: HarperCollins.

Boei, F., Corporaal, A. H., & Van Hunen, W. H. (1989). Describing teacher cognitions with the Repgrid: Some methodological reflections and research findings. In J. Lowyck & C. M. Clark (Eds.), *Teacher thinking and professional action.* Leuven, Belgium: Leuvenarolyn University Press.

Bolin, F. S. (1988). Helping student teachers think about teaching. *Journal of Teacher Education, 39*(2), 48–54.

Borich, G. D. (1994). *Observation skills for effective teaching* (2nd ed.). New York: Macmillan.

Borich, G. D. (2003). *Observation skills for effective teaching* (4th ed.). Upper Saddle River, NJ: Pearson Education.

Boyce, B. A., King, V., & Harris, B. (1993). *The case study approach for pedagogists* (Report No. SP 034 505). Washington, DC: American Alliance for Health, Physical Education, Recreation and Dance. (ERIC Document Reproduction Service No. ED361286)

Brevskolan. (1980). *The study circle: A brief introduction.* Stockholm: Author.

Brock, B. (1990). The principal's role in mentor programs. *Mid-Western Educational Researcher, 12*(4), 18–21.

Brooks, J. G., & Brooks, M. G. (1993). *In search of understanding: The case for constructivist classrooms.* Alexandria, VA: Association for Supervision and Curriculum Development.

Browder, D. M., Schoen, S. F., & Lentz, F. E. (1986–87). Learning to learn through observation. *Journal of Special Education, 20*(4), 447–460.

Brubacher, J. W., Case, C. W., & Reagan, T. G. (1994). *Becoming a reflective educator: How to build a culture of inquiry in the schools.* Thousand Oaks, CA: Corwin.

Bullough, R. V., Jr. (1991). Exploring personal teaching metaphors in preservice teacher education. *Journal of Teacher Education, 42*(1), 43–51.

Bullough, R. V., Jr. (1993). Case records as personal teaching texts for study in preservice teacher education. *Teaching & Teacher Education, 9*(4), 385–396.

Bullough, R. V., Jr. (1994). Analyzing personal teaching metaphors in preservice teacher education as a means for encouraging professional development. *American Educational Research Journal, 31*(1), 197–224.

Bullough, R. V., Jr., & Gitlin, A. D. (2001). *Becoming a student of teaching* (2nd ed.). New York: Routledge Falmer.

Burden, P. R. (1995). *Classroom management and discipline: Methods to facilitate cooperation and instruction.* White Plains, NY: Longman.

Calderhead, J., & Robson, M. (1991). Images of teaching: Student teachers' early conceptions of classroom practice. *Teaching and Teacher Education, 7,* 1–8.

Campbell-Jones, B., & Campbell-Jones, F. (2002). Educating African American children: Credibility at the crossroads. *Educational Horizons, 80*(3), 133–139.

Canter, L., & Canter, M. (1976). *Assertive discipline: A take-charge approach for today's educator.* Los Angeles: Canter and Associates.

Chickering, A. W., & Ehrmann, S. C. (1996, October). Implementing the seven principles: Technology as lever. *AAHE Bulletin,* 3–6.

Chickering, A. W., & Gamson, Z. F. (1991). Applying the seven principles for good practice in undergraduate education. *New directions for teaching and learning, 47,* San Francisco: Jossey-Bass.

Clarke, A. (1995). Professional development in practicum settings: Reflective practice under scrutiny. *Teaching & Teacher Education, 11*(3), 243–261.

Clift, R. T., Houston, W. R., & Pugach, M. C. (Eds.). (1990). *Encouraging reflective practice in education: An analysis of issues and programs.* New York: Teachers College Press.

Cochran-Smith, M., & Lytle, S. L. (1999). The teacher research movement: A decade late. *Educational Researcher, 28,* 15–25.

Cole, A. L., & Knowles, J. G. (2000). *Researching teaching: Exploring practitioner development through reflexive inquiry.* Boston: Allyn & Bacon.

Collier, S. T. (1999). Characteristics of reflective thought during the student teaching experience. *Journal of Practitioner Education, 50*(3), 173–181.

Connelly, F. M., & Clandinin, D. J. (1986). On narrative method, personal philosophy, and narrative unities in the story of teaching. *Journal of Research in Science Teaching, 23*(4), 293–310.

Conway, P. F. (2001). Anticipatory reflection while learning to teach: From a temporally truncated model of reflection in practitioner education. *Teaching and Practitioner Education, 17*(1), 89–106.

Copeland, W. D., Birmingham, C., De La Cruz, E., & Lewin, B. (1993). The reflective practitioner in teaching: Toward a research agenda. *Teaching & Teacher Education, 9*(4), 347–359.

Covey, S. (1989). *The seven habits of highly effective people: Powerful lessons in personal change.* New York: Fireside.

Cruickshank, D. R. (1985). Uses and benefits of reflective teaching. *Phi Delta Kappan, 66*(10), 704–706.

Cruickshank, D. R. (1987). *Reflective teaching: The preparation of students of teaching.* Reston, VA: Association of Teacher Educators.

Cruickshank, D. R., Kennedy, J. J., Williams, E. J., Holton, J., & Fay, D. E. (1981). Evaluation of reflective teaching outcomes. *Journal of Educational Research, 75*(1), 26–31.

Devlin-Scherer, R., & Daly, J. (2001). Living in the present tense: Student teaching telecommunications connect theory and practice. *Journal of Technology and Practitioner Education, 9*(4), 617–634.

Dewey, J. (1933). *How we think.* Boston: DC Heath.

Dobson, J. (1970). *Dare to discipline.* Wheaton, IL: Tyndale House.

Dollase, R. H. (1998). When the state mandates portfolios: The Vermont experience. In N. Lyons (Ed.), *With portfolio in hand: Validating the new practitioner professionalism* (pp. 220–236). New York: Practitioners College Press.

Dutt-Donner, K. M., & Powers, S. (2000). The use of electronic communication to develop alternative avenues for classroom discussion. *Journal of Technology and Practitioner Education, 8*(2), 153–172.

Eby, J. W., & Kujawa, E. (1994). *Reflective planning, teaching, and evaluation: K–12.* New York: Macmillan.

Elbaz, F. (1983). *Thinker thinking: A study of practical knowledge.* London: Croom Helm.

Flake, C. L., Kuhs, T., Donnelly, A., & Ebert, C. (1995). Reinventing the role of teacher: Teacher as researcher. *Phi Delta Kappan, 76*(5), 405–407.

Fosnot, C. T. (1989). *Inquiring teachers, inquiring learners: A constructivist approach for teaching.* New York: Teachers College Press.

Freidus, H. (2000, April). *Fostering reflective practice: Taking a look at context.* Paper presented at the Annual Meeting of the American Educational Research Association, New Orleans, LA.

Fry, E. (1977). Fry's readability graph: Clarifications, validity, and extension to level 17. *Journal of Reading, 21,* 242–252.

Fullan, M. (1991). *The new meaning of educational change.* New York: Teachers College Press.

Garman, N. B. (1986). Reflection, the heart of clinical supervision: A modern rationale for professional practice. *Journal of Curriculum and Supervisor, 2*(1), 1–24.

Giovannelli, M. (2003). Relationship between reflective disposition toward teaching and effective teaching. *Journal of Educational Research, 96*(5), 293–309.

Glasser, W. (1969). *Schools without failure.* New York: Harper & Row.

Glasser, W. (1992). *The quality school: Managing students without coercion* (2nd ed.). New York: HarperPerennial.

Glasser, W. (1993). *The quality school teacher.* New York: HarperPerennial.

Goodnough, K. (2001). Teacher development through action research: A case study of an elementary teacher. *Action in Teacher Education, 23*(1), 37–46.

Gore, J. M., & Zeichner, K. M. (1991). Action research and reflective teaching in preservice teacher education: A case study from the United States. *Teaching & Teacher Education, 7*(2), 119–136.

Grant, G. E. (1992). The sources of structural metaphors in teacher knowledge: Three cases. *Teaching and Teacher Education, 8*(5–6), 433–440.

Grimmett, P. P., MacKinnon, A. M., Erickson, G. L., & Riecken, T. J. (1990). Reflective practice in teacher education. In R. T. Clift, W. R. Houston, & M. C. Pugach (Eds.), *Encouraging reflective practice in education: An analysis of issues and programs* (pp. 20–38). New York: Teachers College Press.

Hagerty, P., Hartman, K., Quate, S., & Seger, D. (1994). *Becoming a teacher researcher: What every classroom teacher should know.* Unpublished manuscript.

Harrington, H. L. (1995). Fostering reasoned decisions: Case-based pedagogy and the professional development of teachers. *Teaching & Teacher Education, 11*(3), 203–214.

Harrington-Macklin, D. (1994). *The team building tool kit—Tips, tactics, and rules for effective workplace teams.* New York: AMACOM.

Hattan, N., & Smith, D. (1994). *Facilitating reflection: Issues and research* (Report No. SP 035 487). Brisbane, Queensland, Australia: Australian Teacher Education Association. (ERIC Document Reproduction Service No. ED375110)

Hattan, N., & Smith, D. (1995). Reflection in teacher education: Towards definition and implementation. *Teaching and Teacher Education, 11*(1), 33–49.

Hawley, W. D. (Ed.). (2002). *The keys to effective schools: Educational reform as continuous improvement.* Thousand Oaks, CA: Corwin.

Heathcote, D. (1980). *Drama as context.* Aberdeen, Scotland, UK: Aberdeen University Press.

Henderson, J. G. (2001). *Reflective teaching: Professional artistry through inquiry* (3rd ed.). Columbus, OH: Merrill/Prentice Hall.

Holt-Reynolds, D. (1991). *The dialogues of teacher education: Entering and influencing pre-service teachers' internal conversations* (Report No. 91–4). Washington, DC: Office of Educational Research and Improvement. (ERIC Document Reproduction Service No. ED337459)

Houston, W. R., & Clift, R. T. (1990). The potential for research contributions to reflective practice. In R. T. Clift, W. R. Houston, & M. C. Pugach (Eds.), *Encouraging reflective practice in education: An analysis of issues and programs* (pp. 208–224). New York: Teachers College Press.

Jacob, E. (1995). Reflective practice and anthropology in culturally diverse classrooms. *The Elementary School Journal, 95*(5), 451–463.

Jankowitz, D. (2003). *The easy guide to repertory grids: A practical guide.* New York: Wiley.

Johnson, G. C. (2003). Accounting for pre-service teachers' use of visual metaphors in narratives. *Educational Administration Abstracts, 28*(1), 3–139.

Johnson, D. W., Johnson, R. T., & Holubec, E. J. (1991). *Cooperation in the classroom* (Rev. ed.). Edina, MN: Interaction.

Joyce, B., & Showers, B. (1995). *Student achievement through staff development: Fundamentals of school renewal* (2nd ed.). White Plains, NY: Longman.

Kagan, D. M. (1992). Professional growth among preservice and beginning teachers. *Review of Educational Research, 62*(2), 129–169.

Kelly, G. (1955). *The psychology of personal constructs: A theory of personality* (Vol. 1). New York: Norton.

Kemmis, S., & McTaggart, R. (1988). *The action research planner* (3rd ed.). Geelong, Australia: Deakin University Press.

Kidder, T. (1989). *Among school children.* New York: Avon.

Kirby, P., & Teddlie, C. (1989). Development of the reflective teaching instrument. *Journal of Research and Development in Education, 22*(4), 45–51.

Kleinfeld, J. (1991). *Wrestling with the angel: What student teachers learn from writing cases* (Report No. SP 033 462). Chicago: American Educational Research Association. (ERIC Document Reproduction Service No. ED347123)

Klenowski, V. (2000). Portfolios: Promoting teaching. *Assessment in Education, 79*(2), 215–236.

Knowles, M. (1990). *The adult learner: A neglected species* (4th ed.). Houston, TX: Gulf.

Korthagen, F. A. J. (1985). Reflective teaching and preservice teacher education in the Netherlands. *Journal of Teacher Education, 36*, 11–15.

Korthagen, F. A. J., & Wubbels, T. (1991, April). *Characteristics of reflective practitioners: Towards an operationalization of the concept of reflection.* Paper presented at the Annual Meeting of the AERA, Chicago.

Kounin, J. S. (1970). *Discipline and group management in classrooms.* New York: Holt, Rinehart & Winston.

Kozol, J. (1991). *Savage inequalities.* New York: Crown.

Kruse, S. D., Louis, K. S., & Bryk, A. S. (1995). An emerging framework for analyzing school-based professional community. In K. S. Louis, S. D. Kruse, & Associates (Eds.), *Professionalism and community: Perspectives on reforming urban schools* (pp. 23–42). Thousand Oaks, CA: Corwin.

Kuit, J. A., Reay, G., & Freeman, R. (2001). Experiences of reflective teaching. *Active Learning in Higher Education 2*(2), 128–142.

Lasley, T. J. (1992). Promoting teacher reflection. *Journal of Staff Development, 13*(1), 24–29.

Levin, B. B. (1995). Using the case method in teacher education: The role of discussion and experience in teachers' thinking about cases. T*eaching & Teacher Education, 11*(1), 63–79.

Levin, J., & Waugh, M. (1998). Teaching teleapprenticeships: Electronic network-based educational frameworks for improving practitioner education. *Journal of Interactive Learning Environments, 6*(1–2), 39–58.

Marshall, C., & Rossman, G. B. (1995). *Designing qualitative research* (2nd ed.). Thousand Oaks, CA: Sage.

McHaney, J. H., & Impey, W. D. (1992). *Strategies for analyzing and evaluating teaching effectiveness using a clinical supervision model* (Report No. TM 019 556). Knoxville, TN: Mid-South Educational Research Association. (ERIC Document Reproduction Service No. ED354268).

Mezirow. J. (1990). *Fostering critical reflection in adulthood: A guide to transformative and emancipatory learning.* San Francisco: Jossey-Bass.

Moore, R. A. (1999). Preservice teachers engaged in reflective classroom research. *The Teacher Educator, 34,* 259–275.

Munby, H. (1982). The place of teachers' beliefs in research on teacher thinking and decision making, and an alternative methodology. *Instructional Science, 11,* 201–225.

Munby, H., & Russell, T. (1989). *Metaphor in the study of teachers' professional language.* Paper presented at the annual meeting of the American Educational Research Association, San Francisco.

National Staff Development Council. (2001). *NSDC Standards.* Retrieved October 6, 2004 from http:www/nsdc.org/standards/index.cfm

Nelsen, J. (1987). *Positive discipline* (2nd ed.). New York: Ballantine.

Noordhoff, K., & Kleinfeld, J. (1990). Shaping the rhetoric of reflection for multicultural settings. In R. T. Clift, W. R. Houston, & M. C. Pugach (Eds.), *Encouraging reflective practice in education: An analysis of issues and programs* (pp. 186–207). New York: Teachers College Press.

Norton, J. L. (1994, February). *Creative thinking and locus of control as predictors of reflective thinking in preservice teachers.* Paper presented at the 74th Annual Meeting of the Association of Teacher Educators, Atlanta, GA.

Oliver, L. P. (1987). *Study circles: Coming together for personal growth and social change.* Washington, DC: Seven Locks.

Olson, J. (1988). Making sense of teaching: Cognition vs. culture. *Journal of Curriculum Studies, 12,* 1–11.

Orlich, D. C., Harder, R. J., Callahan, R. C., Kauchak, D. P., & Gibson, H. W. (1994). *Teaching strategies: A guide to better instruction* (4th ed.). Lexington, MA: DC Heath.

Packard, B. W. (2003). Student training promotes mentoring awareness and action. *The Career Development Quarterly, 51*(4), 335–45.

Palloff, R. M., & Pratt, K. (1999). *Building learning communities in cyberspace: Effective strategies for the online classroom.* San Francisco: Jossey-Bass.

Piaget, J. (1975). *The development of thought: Equilibration of cognitive structures.* New York: Viking.

Posner, G. J. (1996). *Field experience: A guide to reflective teaching* (4th ed.). White Plains, NY: Longman.

Pugach, M. C., & Johnson, L. J. (1990). Developing reflective practice through structured dialogue. In R. T. Clift, W. R. Houston, & M. C. Pugach (Eds.), *Encouraging reflective practice in education: An analysis of issues and programs* (pp. 186–207). New York: Teachers College Press.

Pugh, S. L., Hicks, J. W., Davis, M., & Venstra, T. (1992). *Bridging: A teacher's guide to metaphorical thinking.* Urbana, IL: National Council of Teachers of English.

Redl, F. (1972). *When we deal with children.* New York: Simon & Schuster.

Redl, F., & Wattenberg, W. W. (1959). *Mental hygiene in teaching.* New York: Harcourt Brace.

Risko, V., Roskos, K., & Vukelich, C. (2002). Prospective practitioners' reflection: Strategies, qualities, and perceptions in learning to teach reading. *Reading Research and Instruction, 41*(2), 149–175.

Reis, N. K., & Villaume, S. K. (2002). The benefits, tensions, and visions of portfolios as a wide-scale assessment for practitioner education. *Action in Practitioner Education, 23*(4), 10–17.

Ross, D. D. (1989). First steps in developing a reflective approach. *Journal of Teacher Education, 40*(1), 22–30.

Ross, D. D. (1990). Programmatic structures for the preparation of reflective teachers. In R. T. Clift, W. R. Houston, & M. C. Pugach (Eds.), *Encouraging reflective practice in education: An analysis of issues and programs* (pp. 97–118). New York: Teachers College Press.

Ross, E. W., & Hannay, L. M. (1986). Towards a critical theory of reflective inquiry. *Journal of Teacher Education, 37,* 9–15.

Rumelhart, D. E., & Norman, D. A. (1981). Accretion, tuning, and restructuring: Three modes of learning. In J. W. Cotton & R. Klatzky (Eds.), *Semantic factors in cognition* (pp. 37–60). Hillsdale, NJ: Erlbaum.

Schön, D. A. (1983). *The reflective practitioner.* New York: Basic Books.

Schön, D. A. (1987). *Educating the reflective practitioner: Toward a new design for teaching and learning in the professions.* San Francisco: Jossey-Bass.

Schroeder, M. L. (1996). Lesson design and reflection. *Mathematics Teaching in the Middle School, 1*(18), 648–652.

Scieszka, J. (1989). *The true story of the 3 little pigs!* New York: Viking Penguin.

Shulman, J. (Ed.). (1992). *Case method in teacher education.* New York: Teachers College Press.

Shulman, L. (1998). Teacher portfolios: A theoretical act. In N. Lyons (Ed.), *With portfolio in hand: Validating the new practitioner professionalism.* New York: Practitioners College Press.

Silverman, R., Welty, W. M., & Lyon, S. (1992). *Case studies for teacher problem solving.* New York: McGraw-Hill.

Simmons, J. M., & Sparks, G. M. (1987). *The need for a new model of teacher supervision & evaluation: The implications of identifying reflection as an explicit goal of teacher education programs.* Houston: OERI Conference on Teacher Reflection.

Skinner, B. F. (1971). *Beyond freedom and dignity.* New York: Bantam.

Slavin, R. E. (1983). *Cooperative learning.* New York: Longman.

Smith, H. (2000). The reliability and validity of structural measurers derived from repertory grids. *Journal of Constructivist Psychology, 13*(3), 221–230.

Smith, R. W. (1991). *Obstacles to student teacher reflection: The role of prior school experience as a barrier to teacher development* (Report No. SP 033 243). Chicago: American

Educational Research Association. (ERIC Document Reproduction Service No. ED336352)

Snyder, J., Lippincott, A., & Bower, D. (1998). Portfolios in practitioner education: Technical or transformational. In N. Lyons (Ed.), *With portfolio in hand: Validating the new practitioner professionalism* (pp. 123–142). New York: Practitioners College Press.

Solas, J. (1992). Investigating teacher and student thinking about the process of teaching and learning using autobiography and repertory grid. *Review of Educational Research, 62*(2), 205–225.

Sparks-Langer, G. M., Colton, A. B., Pasch, M., & Starko, A. (1991). *Promoting cognitive, critical, and narrative reflection* (Report No. SP 033 326). Chicago: American Educational Research Association. (ERIC Document Reproduction Service No. ED337435)

Staton, J. (1987). The power of responding in dialogue journals. In T. Fulwiler (Ed.), *The journal book*. Portsmouth, NH: Heinemann.

Stevens, K. (1994). *Aunt Skilly and the stranger*. New York: Ticknor & Fields.

Stivers, J. (1991). *An introduction to case use in teacher education* (Report No. SP 034 030). New York: Confederated Organizations of Colleges for Teacher Education and New York State Association of Teacher Educators. (ERIC Document Reproduction Service No. ED348366)

Tabachnick, B. R., & Zeichner, K. (1984). The impact of the student teaching experience on the development of teacher perspectives. *Journal of Teacher Education, 35*, 28–36.

Taggart, G. L., Phifer, S. J., Nixon, J. A., & Wood, M. (Eds.) (1998). *Rubrics: A handbook for construction and use*. Lanham, MD: Scarecrow Press.

Tillema, H. H. (2000). Belief change towards self-directed learning in student practitioners: Immersion in practice or reflection in action. *Teaching and Practitioner Education, 16*(6), 575–591.

Tillema, H. H., & Kremer-Hayon, L. (2002). "Practicing what we preach"—practitioner educators' dilemmas in promoting self-regulated learning: A cross case comparison. *Teaching and Practitioner Education, 18*(5), 593–607.

Valli, L. (1990). *Teaching as moral reflection: Thoughts on the liberal preparation of teachers* (Report No. SP 033 712). Milwaukee, WI: Association of Independent Liberal Arts Colleges for Teacher Education. (ERIC Document Reproduction Service No. ED344853)

Valli, L. (1997). Listening to other voices: A description of practitioner reflection in the United States. *Peabody Journal of Education, 72*(1), 67–88.

Van Manen, M. (1977). Linking ways of knowing with ways of being practical. *Curriculum Inquiry, 6*(3), 205–228.

Wubbels, T., & Korthagen, F. A. J. (1990). The effects of a pre-service teacher education program for the preparation of reflective teachers. *Journal of Education for Teaching, 16*(1), 29–43.

Yinger, R., & Clark, C. (1981). *Reflective journal writing: Theory and practice* (Occasional Paper No. 50). East Lansing, MI: Institute for Research and Teaching.

Zeichner, K. M. (1987). Preparing reflective teachers: An overview of instructional strategies which have been employed in preservice teacher education. *International Journal of Educational Research, 11*(5), 565–576.

Zeichner, K. M., & Liston, D. P. (1987). Teaching student teachers to reflect. *Harvard Educational Review, 57*, 23–48.

Zinsser, W. (1988). *Writing to learn: How to write and think clearly about any subject at all*. New York: Harper & Row.

# Index

**CORWIN
PRESS**

The Corwin Press logo—a raven striding across an open book—represents the union of courage and learning. Corwin Press is committed to improving education for all learners by publishing books and other professional development resources for those serving the field of K–12 education. By providing practical, hands-on materials, Corwin Press continues to carry out the promise of its motto: **"Helping Educators Do Their Work Better."**